FACES *of*
UNION SOLDIERS
AT SOUTH MOUNTAIN
& HARPERS FERRY

JOSEPH STAHL & MATTHEW BORDERS

THE
History
PRESS

Published by The History Press
Charleston, SC
www.historypress.com

Unless otherwise noted, images are from the private collection of Joseph Stahl.

First published 2021

ISBN 9781540247025

Library of Congress Control Number: 2020951927

Notice: The information in this book is true and complete to the best of our knowledge. It is offered without guarantee on the part of the authors or The History Press. The authors and The History Press disclaim all liability in connection with the use of this book.

To the thirty soldiers whose stories are contained within these pages.

CONTENTS

Acknowledgements

The authors would like to thank the following individuals for their kind assistance in making *Faces of Union Soldiers at South Mountain and Harpers Ferry* possible. As always, our colleagues in the Antietam Battlefield Guides once again enthusiastically supported this research. Specifically, the former chief of the Antietam Guides, Jim Rosebrock, reviewed the manuscript, as did retired guide William Sagle. Both gave advice on how better to flesh out the work and the individuals within. Fellow guide Steven Stotelmyer, a lifelong historian of and advocate for the Battle of South Mountain, helped with the discussion of the ground at the various gaps. Once again, Jim Buchanan was of great assistance in scanning and preparing the soldier CDVs for publication, while Kevin Pawlak reviewed the chapter on Crampton's Gap. Thank you all.

In addition to their fellow guides, Joe and Matt were assisted by Dennis Fry, formerly the chief historian at Harpers Ferry National Historic Site, who reviewed the chapter on Harpers Ferry, providing valuable insight. Thanks, Dennis. Finally, the authors would like to thank The History Press for the opportunity to continue this series. *Faces of Union Soldiers at South Mountain and Harpers Ferry* would not have been possible without Kate Jenkins, our acquisitions editor, who advocated successfully on our behalf to The History Press.

Joe once again had Dr. John Hiller review the work as well. As ever, his insights regarding the flow of the manuscript were invaluable. Dr. Brad Gottfried's excellent troop movement maps of the Maryland Campaign were once again utilized for this work. Thank you, Brad, for not only allowing the use of your fine maps but also taking the time to edit them as needed.

Matt's parents, Drs. Dale and Janet Borders, started his Civil War obsession when he was nine and deserve much credit for his continued passion that led to this book. His mother was particularly helpful assisting in the genealogical research. Further assistance was gained from Mr. Jeffrey Borders and Ms. Chelsie Patterson by their running down grave markers in Ohio. Last but never least, Matt's wife, Kira, was, as ever, supportive of his research by listening patiently as he detailed various uniforms or ranted about trying to find a proper citation. As always, love to you all.

List of Maps

Maryland Campaign

The Gaps

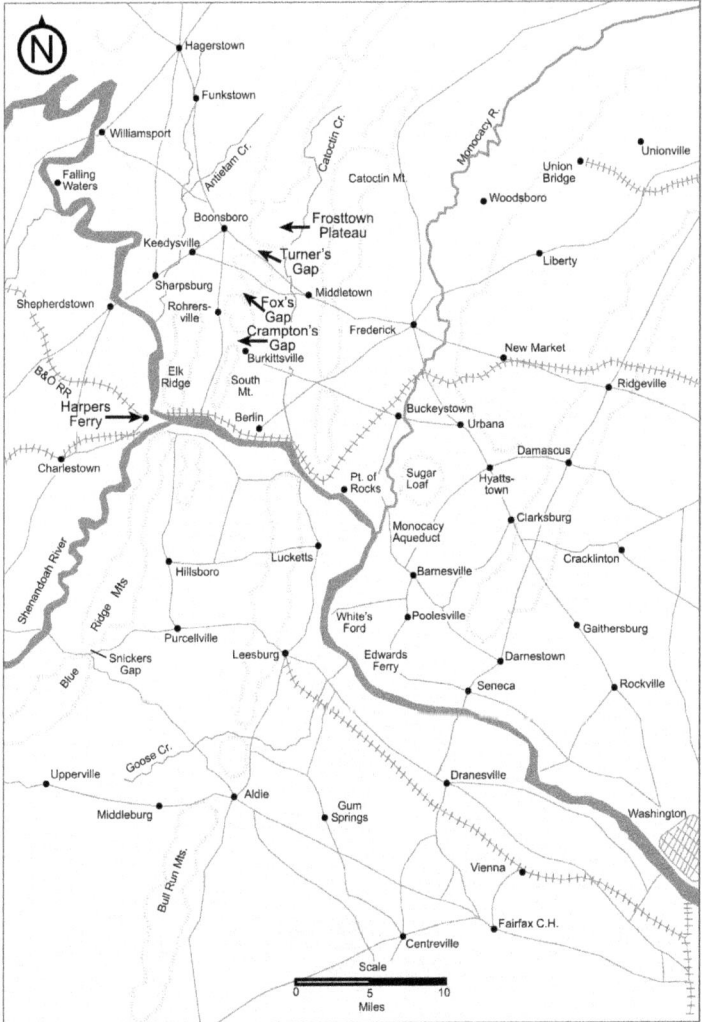

Maryland Campaign—the Gaps. *Map provided by Dr. Bradley Gottfried.*

INTRODUCTION

The purpose of this book is to introduce to the reader a number of individual Union soldiers who fought in the Battles of South Mountain and Harpers Ferry on September 14 and 15, 1862. These are not famous names, and they were not generals at the time of the battle; they were common soldiers attempting to do their duty under trying circumstances. Here you will find their stories—who they were, where they came from and what happened to them. Each soldier's image is included so the reader has a face to go with those stories; the images themselves come from author Joe Stahl's personal collection of *cartes de visite*. The soldiers' units and their locations on the field are presented using maps provided with permission from Brad Gottfried's book *The Maps of Antietam*. The time stamps on these maps and the descriptions of the events that these units were involved in are based on information obtained in *The War of the Rebellion: A Compilation of the Official Records of the Union and Confederate Armies* and their individual unit histories.

We hope that readers will use this book as they tour these battlefield landscapes. However, it must be noted that many locations where the fighting took place are not accessible to the public, as the ground is in private hands. On South Mountain, portions of Turner's and Fox's Gaps and part of South Mountain State Park are accessible by trails and feature monuments and interpretive signs. Crampton's Gap is even more accessible; with the town of Burkittsville, Maryland, at its base, it is possible to follow the same roads that led to the gap, what is today Gathland State Park. The least accessible gap in South Mountain is Frosttown Gap. This isolated location is almost entirely in private hands. While the area of much of the fighting can still be driven through on the public roads, there are no public trails or accessibility. Fortunately, Harpers Ferry National Historic Site in Harpers Ferry, West Virginia, offers numerous trails, markers and in-depth history on the fighting that occurred around the famous town in September 1862.

We encourage visitors to these sites to get out of their vehicles and see the ground where these soldiers fought. Walking this terrain helps to make the events of more than 155 years ago all the more real. For the truly ambitious, there is also the option of hiking through much of this battlefield landscape using the Appalachian Trail. Running from Washington Monument State Park, the Appalachian Trail passes through Turner's, Fox's and Crampton's Gaps along the spine of South Mountain before heading down to the Potomac River and over to Harpers Ferry. While the fighting for the South Mountain gaps and Harpers Ferry occurred during the same period of time, this book is not set up chronologically. Instead, the chapters follow the action from the northernmost gap, Frosttown, south to Harpers Ferry. The intent is to aid the reader and battlefield visitor in visiting these locations and reduce the amount of backtracking that would occur otherwise.

CARTE DE VISITE (CDV)

Carte de visite is French for "visiting card." By 1860, these paper images had become common in the United States. Since the price was within reach for many people ($2.50 to $3.00 per dozen), it was not unusual to have an album of images of the family and relatives. The cameras of the era took four images from four lenses at one time. The glass negative could produce multiple copies, which accounted for the low price. The images were then pasted onto a card to make them sturdier; this was done for all CDVs at the time, and a lack of a seam can be a good indicator for determining if an image is a modern reproduction. These images became very popular with soldiers, allowing them to show off their uniforms, leave a keepsake for someone at home or give a copy to a comrade.

Some of the CDVs included in this work have a stamp on the back of them. From August 1, 1864, to August 1, 1866, the images were taxed by the Federal government and required a revenue stamp on the reverse of the card (this helps in dating some cards). The tax was to help raise revenue for the war effort: two cents on photographs under twenty-five cents, three cents on photos up to fifty cents and five cents for those costing up to one dollar. Photos were to be canceled—usually by having a line drawn through the stamp, with the photographer's initials and the date of the sale—but sadly this regulation was often ignored, and the stamps were either struck out or rubber-stamped for convenience.[1] By the 1880s, other sizes of photographs had begun to replace the CDV in popularity.

We have also included a description of each soldier's image to discuss the details that can be made out in each CDV. Specifics such as uniform features, rank and other aspects of the images are discussed. It is hoped that these details will help readers see these men as the individuals they were and not just faces from a bygone era.

THE MARYLAND CAMPAIGN OF 1862

By the fall of 1862, the American Civil War had been raging for nearly a year and a half. Thousands had fallen on both sides, and the fortunes of war had swayed back and forth. The previous spring, Federal forces under the command of Major General George B. McClellan had attempted to take the heart out of the rebellion by capturing the Confederate capital of Richmond, Virginia. A slow-going but persistent campaign moving up the Virginia Peninsula between the York and James Rivers succeeded in driving Confederate defenders to the outskirts of Richmond. It was during this desperate fighting before the Confederate capital that General Robert E. Lee was given command of Confederate forces following the Battle of Seven Pines, fought May 31–June 1, 1862. Consolidating his forces, Lee soon launched the blistering counteroffensive known as the Seven Days. Although costly in manpower to the Confederates, this series of offensive battles convinced the Union Army of the Potomac to fall back to its fortified base of supply at Harrison's Landing on the James River.

With Federal forces concentrated at Harrison's Landing, Lee chose not to attack. Instead, he shifted north, opening the Northern Virginia Campaign against Union forces under the command of Major General John Pope. The climax of this campaign saw Pope's Union Army of Virginia defeated at the Second Battle of Bull Run (Second Manassas), fought August 28–30. With Federal forces now withdrawn from Harrison's Landing and Pope's army sent fleeing back to the defenses of Washington, Lee saw an opportunity. With an open road north, Lee's Army of Northern

Virginia crossed the Potomac River into the border state of Maryland on September 4, 1862.

The first Confederate invasion of the North was a bold move but also a risky one. Lee's army was battle hardened and confident, but it had also been worn down by a season of campaigning. Lee's communications with Confederate President Jefferson Davis laid out some of his thoughts on why he chose to take this risk, including resupplying his army off the farmlands of Maryland, keeping the pressure on Washington and keeping the Federals out of war-ravaged Northern Virginia as long as possible.[2]

Additionally, the political ramifications of Lee's invasion made this move very tempting. Many in the Confederacy believed that Maryland was being forcibly held in the Union, although both houses of the Maryland Assembly had determined that they did not have the legal authority to leave the Union as early as April 27, 1861.[3] It was thought that all that would need to happen was for Lee's army to enter the state and Marylanders would flock to the Confederate banner. This was not the case, however, as Lee had entered Maryland in the central part of the state and moved through the western portion, areas that were decidedly unionist in their sympathies.

It was also hoped that Confederate action in a Northern state could lead to more peace-leaning Democrats to be elected during the 1862 elections. This could have potentially led to a negotiated peace between the two sides. Finally, the ever-looming shadow of Europe and the threat of intervention by a foreign power weighed on the Lincoln administration. If Lee could win again, this time on Northern soil, it could be enough to convince the British and or the French to recognize the Southern states as an independent nation and intercede on their behalf.[4] Thus the stakes were incredibly high when Lee chose to cross the Potomac near Leesburg, Virginia, in early September.

The Federal response to this invasion was dramatic. Major General McClellan was given command of all Federal forces in and around Washington. The recently defeated Union Army of Virginia was dissolved and its forces added to a reorganizing Army of the Potomac. Additional troops were taken from the forts around Washington, although the capital was still left heavily defended. By September 7, 1862, this amalgamation of forces stepped off in pursuit of the Confederates. McClellan's orders were straightforward: he was to take his still reorganizing command, move into Western Maryland and drive Lee out, all while keeping Washington and Baltimore protected.[5]

The Federal pursuit across Maryland was more aggressive than Lee had anticipated. Meanwhile, on September 9, 1862, Robert E. Lee dictated

Special Orders 191, which divided his army. Major General Thomas J. "Stonewall" Jackson, along with several other divisions, was sent back to the Potomac River to compel the abandonment of the Federal outpost at Harpers Ferry or force the garrison to surrender. The presence of the Federals along Lee's line of communication and supply could not be ignored. The rest of the Army of Northern Virginia, under Major General James Longstreet, and the portion with which Lee was traveling, continued westward toward Hagerstown, Maryland. The intention was that once the action at Harpers Ferry was concluded, the army was to consolidate at Hagerstown. At this point, it could move where it liked, either choosing ground on which to meet the Federal pursuit or move farther north into Pennsylvania. This order was implemented on September 10 but was complicated three days later when Federal troops pursuing Lee found an extra copy that had been made and subsequently lost. With this information in hand, General McClellan had confirmation of the reports that the Confederate army was divided and that Harpers Ferry was threatened.[6] He had ordered his forces to advance, hoping to get in between the separate commands of the Army of Northern Virginia and destroy it in detail.

This pursuit of Confederate forces led to the desperate engagements at South Mountain and Harpers Ferry in mid-September 1862. The thirty men presented here were part of this pursuit and the opening battles of the Maryland Campaign. The fighting to come, and their sacrifices in it, was to be the prelude to an even worse bloodletting on the banks of Antietam Creek on September 17, 1862. Combined, these battles made up some of the worst fighting in the American Civil War but helped to ensure the defeat of the first Confederate invasion of the North, a major turning point in the war, and the beginning of a new birth of freedom for more than 4 million enslaved people.

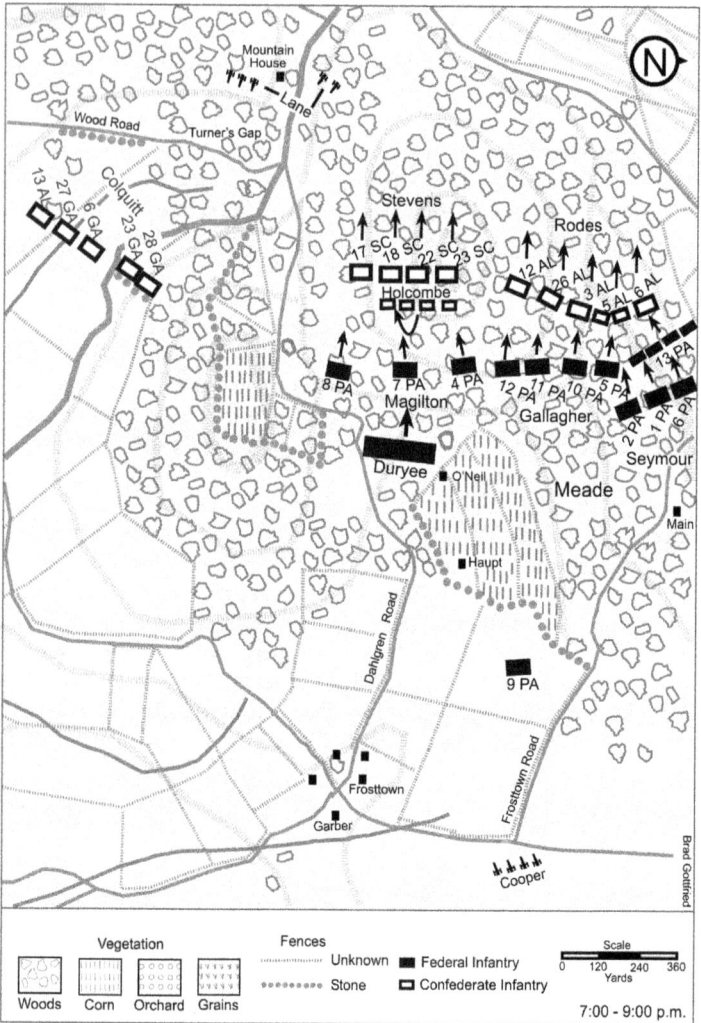

South Mountain—Frosttown Plateau, 7:00 p.m.–9:00 p.m. *Map provided by Dr. Bradley Gottfried.*

Chapter 1

FROSTTOWN GAP

Late in the afternoon of Sunday, September 14, 1862, Brigadier General George Meade's Division of Pennsylvania Reserves regiments approached Frosttown Gap. This was the northernmost of the four gaps in South Mountain attacked by the Army of the Potomac that day and was known by a variety of names during this period, including Frosttown Gap and Frosttown Plateau. General Meade deployed his three brigades, with Brigadier General Truman Seymour's 1st Brigade on the right of the division. Colonel Thomas Gallagher's 3rd Brigade deployed in the middle, and Colonel Albert Magilton's 2nd Brigade was on the left as the units advanced up the ridge toward the gap. The map shows the positions of the units around 7:00 p.m. to 9:00 p.m. On the extreme right was the 6th Pennsylvania Reserve, belonging to Seymour's Brigade; the regiment was commanded by Colonel William Sinclair. To their left was the 5th Pennsylvania Reserves regiment, also from Seymour's Brigade. Farther to the left was the 12th Pennsylvania Reserves of Gallagher's Brigade. Finally, the 4th, 7th and 8th Pennsylvania Reserves regiments of Magilton's Brigade held the left of the division and succeeded in advancing the farthest toward the Frosttown Gap.

In his report of the battle, General Meade described the movements of his division:

> The division left its camp at Monocacy early on the morning of the 14th instant, and marched to Middletown [Maryland] beyond, where it was halted about 1 p.m. of that day.... The enemy was disputing our passage

over the turnpike though the South Mountain, and had been attacked on the left by General Reno. After some consultation with the general commanding the right wing and the corps, I was directed to move the division on a road leading off to the right of the turnpike and toward the enemy's left. After advancing over a mile on this road, the division…was turned across the field to the left, and moved to an advantageous position to support [Captain James] *Cooper's battery.*[7]

General Meade's Division consisted entirely of the famous Pennsylvania Reserves. The reserves were regiments that were raised beyond the initial quota requested of the State of Pennsylvania. On May 15, 1861, Pennsylvania authorized the forming of the "Reserve Volunteer Corps of the Commonwealth,"[8] consisting of the 30th to 44th Pennsylvania regiments, thirteen of which were infantry. Having yet to be called for by the Federal government, these regiments were numbered the 1st through 13th Pennsylvania Reserves, names they continued to use long after they were given their state designations. A quick way to determine the official state number of a Pennsylvania Reserves regiment is to take their reserve number and add twenty-nine, the number of regiments that existed prior to the reserves being formed. All six of the following soldiers were members of the Pennsylvania Reserves.

35TH PENNSYLVANIA INFANTRY / 6TH PENNSYLVANIA RESERVES

The 35th Pennsylvania Infantry, better known as the 6th Reserves, was composed of men from all parts of the state. The regiment was mustered into service at Washington for three years on July 27, 1861. The 6th Pennsylvania Reserves' first taste of combat was at Dranesville, Virginia, in December 1861, after which it took part in the Peninsula Campaign in the spring of 1862. That fall, the 6th Pennsylvania Reserves suffered severely due to the Battles of Second Bull Run, South Mountain, Antietam and Fredericksburg. Following the Mud March in the winter of 1863, the 6th Pennsylvania Reserves was pulled off the line until the Gettysburg Campaign, where it was once again heavily engaged. The 6th Pennsylvania Reserves continued to serve into the Overland Campaign in the spring of 1864, its final battle being Totopotomoy Creek. Returning to Harrisburg, Pennsylvania, the regiment was mustered out on June 11,

1864. New recruits and veterans who reenlisted were transferred to the 191st Pennsylvania Infantry.[9]

Colonel William Sinclair, commanding the 6th Pennsylvania Reserves, discussed only the fighting at Antietam and did not mention the action at South Mountain in his after-action report. However, Brigadier General Seymour did write a report describing the actions of the regiments in his brigade, including the 6th Pennsylvania Reserves: "[T]he hill won, and many prisoners taken. Looking to the left, an extended field of corn led directly to the main position on the mountain itself. The First, Second, and Fifth changed direction, and, supported by the Sixth in column of companies, continued the attack. A few volleys were fired, bayonets were leveled, three hearty cheers given, and the whole line moved quickly up the hillside with an impetus that drove the enemy from cover and gave us the crest in time to anticipate a fresh brigade which was advancing to support their line, but which then turned in retreat."[10]

At South Mountain, the 6th Pennsylvania Reserves reported losses of eleven enlisted men killed, one officer and forty-two enlisted men wounded and no missing, for a total of fifty-four casualties due to the fighting at Frosttown Gap.[11]

In Company A of the 6th Pennsylvania Reserves was Lieutenant Albion B. Jamison from Columbia County. Jamison mustered into the regiment as a second sergeant on April 22, 1861, for three years of service. His service records state that at the time of his enlistment, Albion Jamison was twenty-five years old and five feet, six inches tall, with dark hair, gray eyes and a light complexion. Prior to the war, he had worked as a clerk and was born in Columbia County. On October 23, 1861, Albion was elected first sergeant of his company. In his records, his status of being present or otherwise was "not stated" through December 31, 1861, as was common in the early service records. Albion was "present" starting in January/February 1862; however, a note in the records says that during the period of May/June, he was sick at the Cliffburne General Hospital in Washington, D.C. Lieutenant Jamison returned to duty in July/August and was present at both the Battle of South Mountain and Antietam. Although he fought through Frosttown Gap without incident, he later injured himself by "jumping from a fence, at the battle of Antietam September 17, 1862, causing an aneurism of the popliteal artery, (since obliterated) and an injury to the tendon of the extensor muscles of the thigh."[12] Eventually, this injury resulted in Albion being sent to Kingston USA General Hospital in Washington on January 19, 1863. Albion returned to the 6th Pennsylvania Reserves and was promoted to first lieutenant on April 24, 1863. Almost two months later, he was appointed quartermaster on June 13. During July/August, he claimed that he was owed an extra ten dollars per month as quartermaster. On November 4, 1863, Lieutenant Jamison was absent on sick leave once more due to synovitis, or inflammation of the knee joint, likely from his fence jumping at Antietam. Albion returned to the regiment on January 6, 1864, and was present until his muster out on June 11, 1864. He was last paid on February 29, 1864. He was awarded a brevet promotion to captain on March 13, 1865, for "Gallant and Meritorious Service in the Wilderness Campaign."[13] Following the war, Jamison attended medical school at the University of Georgetown, graduating on March 5, 1867.[14] According to his pension card, Albion Jamison filed for a pension on April 28, 1888, and died on May 29, 1920, in Washington, D.C.[15]

THIS PHOTOGRAPH OF ALBION B. Jamison was taken at the Plumb Gallery in Washington, D.C., by photographer B.P. Paige. A previous collector has identified First Lieutenant Albion Jamison but has used the more modern spelling of his last name, which can also be seen in the family genealogy.[16] This image has little in the way of decoration—only a chair and a carpet with a blank wall behind to focus the attention on Jamison himself. The gallery provided the lieutenant with a brace to keep his head steady during the exposure of the shot. The base of the brace can be seen between his legs and just behind Jamison.

This standing view provides numerous details of Lieutenant Jamison's uniform. His footwear, however, is mostly hidden, making it hard to determine if he is wearing boots or shoes, more commonly known as bootees at the time. In either case, these would have been private purchase, as officers were not issued uniforms and had to provide their own.[17] The rather blunt toe suggests a shoe of some type, while the shine implies a higher-quality smooth leather surface. Covering the top of his footwear are Jamison's dark-blue trousers, the color of the regular army before the Civil War; dark-blue trousers were worn by officers and the regulars even after General Orders No. 108, which established the use of light-blue kersey wool trousers for both officers and enlisted men.[18]

Lieutenant Jamison's dark-blue frock coat begins at the top of his knees with the long skirting that these formal coats are known for. Unlike the frock coats issued to the enlisted men, an officer's frock was not as form fitting and had significantly more fabric in the sleeves.[19] The three small cuff buttons

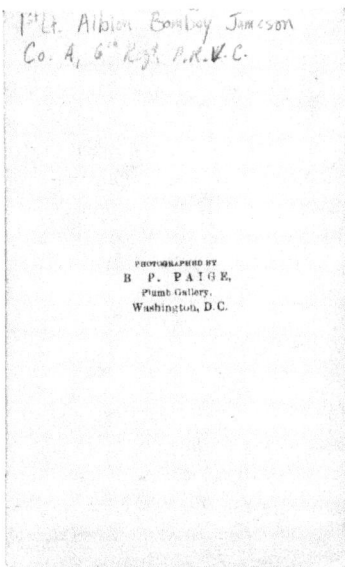

Left: Lieutenant Albion B. Jamison, 6th Pennsylvania Reserves. *Right*: Back of Jamison's image.

on each wrist are also indications of an officer's frock coat. In this case, the buttons on Jamison's left sleeve can just barely be made out, while those on his right wrist can easily be seen as he has placed his hand into the internal breast pocket of the frock coat. Of course, the shoulder boards on Jamison's frock are the most obvious indicator of rank—gold embroidered with a single gold bar at each end to show he is a first lieutenant. As the 6th Pennsylvania Reserves was an infantry regiment, the interior color of the shoulder board should be light blue, for the infantry. However, Jamison had been made the quartermaster of the regiment, a staff position, thus his boards have the deep blue interior of the regimental command staff.[20] Running down the front of his frock are nine large buttons, six of which can be seen at least in part. It is difficult to determine if these are the usual Federal eagle buttons or Pennsylvania state seal buttons—either design is possible.

In Lieutenant Jamison's left hand is his kepi. The short-brimmed, French-inspired hat was found in many different styles throughout the armies of the Civil War. This particular kepi, though, is a bit rarer. Picking up the light from the flash it becomes clear that this kepi is made of oil cloth and was intended to be used as a rain hat.[21]

To finish off his appearance, Lieutenant Jamison has on what appears to be a new paper collar for his shirt, its edges coming up just over the collar of his frock. He has also taken care of his facial hair, trimming his mustache and neatly combing his hair, perhaps applying some sort of haircare product as well. Not only did this provide for a better image, but it also conformed to regulations on appearance in the army.[22]

34TH PENNSYLVANIA INFANTRY / 5TH PENNSYLVANIA RESERVES

The 5th Pennsylvania Reserves was recruited in the counties of Centre, Lancaster, Huntingdon, Lycoming, Northumberland, Clearfield, Union and Bradford. Recruits were ordered to report at Camp Curtin, near Harrisburg, Pennsylvania, where on June 20, 1861, the regiment was organized. The next day, the 5th Pennsylvania Reserves along with the 13th Pennsylvania Reserves and Battery A, 1st Pennsylvania Artillery, were ordered to Cumberland, Maryland, to support the 11th Indiana Infantry, then stationed there. The regiment's soldiers spent their time on guard, occasionally skirmishing with Confederate cavalry before being ordered back to Harrisburg following the Union defeat at Bull Run on July 21, 1861.[23] In early August, the Reserves regiments were massed at Tennallytown, in the District of Columbia, and were organized as Brigadier General George A. McCall's Division of the Army of the Potomac. The 5th Pennsylvania Reserves was assigned to the 1st Brigade of the division. McCall's Division of Pennsylvania Reserves went on to fight throughout 1862, on the Peninsula, at Second Bull Run, in the Maryland Campaign and finally at Fredericksburg. With the rest of the Pennsylvania Reserves, they were ordered to the defenses of Washington in February 1863 and remained there until the Gettysburg Campaign. Following the pursuit of the Army of Northern Virginia, the 5th Pennsylvania Reserves wintered in Alexandria, Virginia. With the opening of the Overland Campaign in the spring of 1864, the Pennsylvania Reserves participated in multiple battles until the end of May. On May 31, 1864, the term of service of the 5th Pennsylvania Reserves expired. Along with other Reserves regiments, it was relieved from duty and ordered back to Harrisburg, where on June 11 the 5th Pennsylvania Reserves was mustered out of service. Those veterans who had reenlisted and its recruits were transferred to the 191st Pennsylvania Infantry.[24]

The commander of the 5th Pennsylvania Reserves, Colonel Joseph W. Fisher, stated the following in his report on the fighting at South Mountain:

> *On Sunday, 14th instant, my regiment was ordered by you* [General Seymour] *to take a position on the north side of a hill, a spur of the South Mountain, in the good old State of Maryland, near the Monocacy, and charge the enemy through a corn-field on the northern slope, go to the top of the hill, and hold it, and be sure to kill some of the rebels. In the march my regiment was the fourth in the brigade. I followed the skirmishers of the First Pennsylvania Rifles. On arriving on the summit of the first hill I discovered that the Rifles* [13th Pennsylvania Reserves] *were engaged with a body of the enemy, which was giving them an undue share of the work. I then changed direction and marched by the left flank, where I gave them (the rebels) a raking fire, punishing them severely and causing them to break and retreat in great disorder. I at once pursued them over a high stonewall and through a corn-field, reaching the top of the hill before either of the other regiments, all the time keeping my line in perfect order. When I arrived at the summit I halted, called my rolls, and found only eight of my men unaccounted for. In this fight I lost 1 killed (John A. Hougendoubler, of Company K, a gallant and faithful soldier, who in seventeen months' service has not to my knowledge ever had to be reproved by his company or regimental commander), and 12 wounded. I wish to ask particular attention to the fact that although my regiment had been several hours engaged, I had but eight men absent at my evening roll-call.*[25]

On June 21, 1861, John Woods Russell mustered into Company A of the 5th Pennsylvania Reserves as a sergeant for three years of service. Russell stated that he was nineteen years old. His service records show he was the "4th Sergeant" and "present" starting on June 21 through October 1861. The November/December report lists him as "not stated." After that period, Russell was present until his wounding in 1864. The next event in his service records was his promotion to first sergeant on August 1, 1862, the rank he held at the Battle of South Mountain. Seven months later, Sergeant Russell was promoted again to second lieutenant on March 6, 1863. In the winter of 1864, Russell was granted a ten-day leave starting on February 14, 1864. After his return, Lieutenant Russell was wounded on May 5, 1864, during the Battle of the Wilderness. His injury was described as a gunshot wound to the head.[26] It is interesting to note that a brief article covering the return of

Lieutenant Russell's body to Pennsylvania described his wounding and when it occurred differently from his service records:

> *The body of J. Woods Russel* [Russell], *of Brady township, in this county* [Union] *was brought home for burial on the 26th inst. Lieut. R. belonged to the 5th Pa. Reserves, Co. A. He enlisted as a private, in May, 1861, at Jersey Shore, and was in all the hard-fought battles in which the 5th participated. He was promoted ten months ago; was wounded on the 10th inst., by a small fragment of shell penetrating the brain, in the battle near Spottsylvania Court House, and was brought to the Hospital at Alexandria but died there on the 22nd. Lieut. Russel was only 22 years of age, of excellent character, and is mourned by all who knew him.*[27]

As stated in the newspaper, he had been taken to the Third Division U.S. General Hospital at either Grosvenor House or the Grosvenor Branch Hospital in Alexandria, Virginia, on May 14, 1864. Sadly, Lieutenant Russell died as a result of his wound on May 22, 1864. The inventory of his possessions in his file shows: one coat, one pair trousers, two cotton shirts, one blanket, one bunch of keys, one pair boots, one pair stockings, one sword and belt, two photographs, sundry pocket articles and five dollars in notes.[28] John Woods Russell was laid to rest at the Washington Presbyterian Church Cemetery, Union County, Pennsylvania.[29]

THE IMAGE OF JOHN Woods Russell was taken some time after his promotion to second lieutenant in March 1863. At that time, the 5th Pennsylvania Reserves was stationed in the defenses of the national capital, and the lieutenant would have had ample opportunity to get away to the city to have this image made. This particular CDV was taken at the gallery of R.W. Addis on Pennsylvania Avenue. Russell may have intended this as a calling card, as he signed the back with his rank and regiment. In addition, at least two previous collectors have written on the back of the image. The first, just under Russell's signature, wrote out Russell's name, company and regiment, along with his date of death and cause of death. The other collector, in very light pencil, wrote along the right edge simply, "Killed May 8 1864," which is incorrect. The Addis gallery provided a chair for Lieutenant Russell to steady himself, as well as a brace to help keep the head still during the exposure. The base of the brace can be seen between his feet and just behind him.

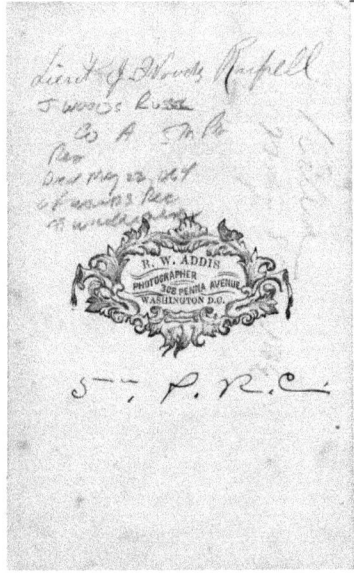

Left: Sergeant John Woods Russell, 5th Pennsylvania Reserves. *Right*: Back of Russell's image.

For this standing view, John Woods Russell has footwear of an indeterminate type, although the tapering toe does suggest a private purchase boot. His dark-blue trousers are those worn by an infantry officer; the eighth-of an-inch light-blue piping signifying the infantry can just be seen running up his left leg near the knee.[30] Starting at the top of the knee is the long skirting on Russell's frock coat. The coat is worn open for this image, only the topmost of its nine buttons being closed. Under his coat, however, can be seen his dark-blue officer's vest, with seven of its nine buttons visible. As the shirt was considered an undergarment, the vest allowed for the coat to be open for greater comfort and ventilation while still in polite company. Having the single button closed at the collar also allowed Russell to conform to regulations.[31] The cuff buttons on the officer's frock can be seen along his left wrist, while on his shoulders are the most obvious badges of rank, his shoulder boards. Being a second lieutenant of infantry, Lieutenant Russell's gold embroidered shoulder boards were on a piece of light-blue cloth, with no further decoration in the interior.[32]

In addition to his uniform, John Woods Russell is also wearing a cravat, which can be seen just above his coat collar. This small tie is actually mentioned in the regulations, and officers were only allowed to wear black cravats while in uniform.[33] In this case, Russell has tied the cravat around the new paper collar that was attached to his shirt. Another personal touch is the small pinkie ring that can be seen on his left hand. Finally, Russell has trimmed his mustache and swept his unruly hair back, making for a rather rakish-looking image.

41ˢᵀ PENNSYLVANIA INFANTRY / 12ᵀᴴ PENNSYLVANIA RESERVES

The 41ˢᵗ Pennsylvania, known as the 12ᵗʰ Pennsylvania Reserves, was organized at Camp Curtin near Harrisburg on July 25, 1861. The regiment was retained by the State of Pennsylvania after the other Pennsylvania Reserves regiments were ordered elsewhere. The 12ᵗʰ Pennsylvania Reserves' first duty was guarding the state arsenal in Harrisburg in late July from a rumored attack. Following this brief duty, the regiment was mustered into the service of the United States for three years on August 10, 1861. In August, it reported at the camp of the Reserves in Tennallytown, and was attached to the 3ʳᵈ Brigade.[34] The regiment remained in the 3ʳᵈ Brigade through the campaigns of 1862, including the Peninsula, Second Bull Run, the Maryland Campaign and Fredericksburg. The 12ᵗʰ Pennsylvania Reserves wintered in the defenses of Washington until it was detached to Catlett's Station in April 1863. Afterward, the regiment took the field again for the Gettysburg Campaign, as well as at Bristoe Station and Mine Run. Wintering at Catlett's Station, the 12ᵗʰ Pennsylvania Reserves participated the next spring in the 1864 Overland Campaign. The Battle of Bethesda Church, also known as Totopotomoy Creek, during the Overland Campaign was the 12ᵗʰ Pennsylvania Reserves' final engagement. Ordered home to Harrisburg, the regiment was mustered out on June 11, 1864. Those veterans who had reenlisted and recruits were transferred to the 190ᵗʰ Pennsylvania Infantry for the rest of their service.[35]

Interestingly, the 12ᵗʰ Pennsylvania Reserves report from both South Mountain and Antietam was written by Captain Andrew J. Bolar. However, the commanding officer for the regiment at both those engagements was Captain Richard M. Gustin, who took over the regiment following the wounding of Colonel Martin D. Hardin at Second Bull Run.[36] In Bolar's official report of the actions on September 14, he stated:

Frosttown Gap

[T]he Third Brigade was ordered into line of battle in view of the enemy, posted in hidden position on the mountain. During the time the line was being formed the regiment was exposed to shell and canister from a rebel battery on the hill, which fortunately did but little execution. At the command "advance" the Twelfth Regiment, on the left of the brigade, marched forward, crossed a small ravine and entered the mountain, under fire of the enemy, who could not be seen until we had come into close quarters. The regiment went on up the mountain without halting. The progress was slow on account of the steepness of the hill and the rocks, logs, and brush with which the ground was covered. The firing was incessant on both sides, the rebels yielding the ground only when routed out of their hidden positions by the balls and bayonets of our men. The musketry was constant from the base to the top of the mountain. The regiment was somewhat broken when it arrived at the top of the mountain, in consequence of the roughness of the ground and the weariness of the men.[37]

At South Mountain, the 12th Pennsylvania Reserves reported losses of six enlisted killed, one officer and eighteen enlisted wounded and no missing, for a total of twenty-five.[38]

Fighting up South Mountain in Company C was Corporal John G. Rohm (maybe a private, as records are confused). He was mustered into the service for three years on August 10, 1861, as a private in Company K. John was twenty-one at the time of his enlistment and stated that he was living in Bradford County, Pennsylvania. In his service records, starting on October 31, John is shown as a corporal, and his status was "not stated," which was common early in the war. Corporal Rohm was "present" starting with the January/February report. However, the report for July/August shows that John was now a private and transferred to Company C as of July 20, 1862. John was listed as "Wounded in Action on September 17, 1862," but nothing further is in his records. It must not have been serious, as he was listed as "present" on subsequent rolls until his muster-out date. On April 20, 1863, John was promoted to second lieutenant and was mustered as an officer on May 1, 1863. Late that year, John was given leave to visit his dying sister November 14–22 by order of General Meade. Lieutenant Rohm was mustered out of service on June 11, 1864; he had last been paid on February 29, 1864. At his mustering out, John was also due a bounty of $100. On March 13, 1865, Lieutenant Rohm was brevetted first lieutenant, for special gallantry at Mine Run, Virginia.[39] According to his pension card, John Rohm died on July 4, 1867, and his widow later received a pension.[40]

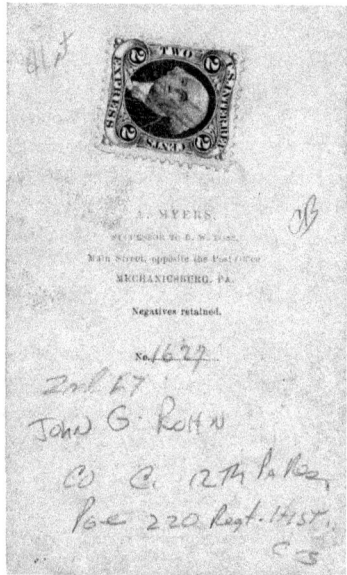

Left: Corporal (maybe a private, records are confused) John G. Rohm, 12th Pennsylvania Reserves. *Right*: Back of Rohm's image.

LIKELY TAKEN AFTER HIS mustering out of service, this image was made at the A. Myers gallery in Mechanicsburg, Pennsylvania, just a few miles outside Harrisburg. As the 12th Pennsylvania Reserves mustered out of service in June 1864, the luxury tax on CDVs had not yet gone into effect. It is possible that this image was taken at a later date, as the tax stamps were utilized to help raise revenue from August 1864 through August 1866. The two-cent stamp used here was for images that cost less than twenty-five cents.[41] It is also possible that this is a reprint, as the photographer kept the negatives and, in this case, has made note of the number. Lieutenant John Rohm could have been through the area late in 1863 when he was visiting his dying sister and had the image taken during that trip. Along with the tax stamp and photographer's information, a previous collector jotted down some details about John Rohm in pencil. His name, rank, company and regiment are listed, along with a reference to the 12th Pennsylvania Reserves unit history; this same CDV is featured on one of the illustration pages in that work.[42]

As for the image itself, the gallery provided a number of props for Lieutenant John Rohm's CDV. There is a chair barely in the frame, as well as a decorative floor cover of some type. A large drapery comes down the left side of the image, and a small table with book has been provided to lean on. The book appears to have clasps and could be a Bible or even a photo album. As with most standing views, a brace has also been provided to keep Rohm's head steady; its base can just be seen behind his right leg.

Lieutenant John Rohm's footwear has seen more wear than those of the previous officers. These are lacking any polish and may even be a bit muddy. They are probably boots or perhaps private purchase shoes. Rohm's trousers are the light- or sky blue kersey wool trousers utilized by the Federal army after December 1861 and have the eighth-of-an-inch dark-blue piping running up the seam that signified an infantry officer.[43] In addition, Rohm's frock coat is typical of an officer's variant, with its long skirting coming to the knee, as well as more voluminous sleeves. One of the cuff buttons can just be seen by his left hand. The nine buttons running down the frock are open, except for the topmost, and are probably Federal eagle buttons. Underneath the frock, seven buttons, of what is likely a nine-button officer's vest, can be seen.[44] Rohm has also opened three of his vest buttons, likely for ventilation, and his white shirt can just be made out both there and around his neck. As a symbol of rank, his shoulder boards are clearly visible, and as he is a second lieutenant, there is no additional decoration within them. Finally, Rohm's hair has been neatly combed, and he is sporting a wonderful set of mutton chops for his image.

33RD PENNSYLVANIA INFANTRY / 4TH PENNSYLVANIA RESERVES

The 33rd Pennsylvania Infantry, better known as the 4th Pennsylvania Reserves, was sent to Camp Washington in Easton, Pennsylvania, for organizing and training before being mustered in on June 21, 1861, to serve for three years.[45] The regiment left for Baltimore, Maryland, on July 21 and remained there until the end of August, when it was ordered to Tennallytown. As part of the 2nd Brigade of Pennsylvania Reserves, the regiment was active throughout the Peninsula Campaign in the spring of 1862, as well at Second Bull Run, South Mountain, Antietam and Fredericksburg. Following the heavy fighting in 1862, the 4th Pennsylvania Reserves was ordered to the defenses of Washington to recuperate. During the winter of 1863, the 2nd

Brigade, including the 4th Pennsylvania Reserves, became part of the XXII Corps and remained in the defenses of Washington until January 1864. The regiment was then ordered to West Virginia to picket Martinsburg. Though unsuccessful in running down Confederate forces in the area, the 4th Pennsylvania Reserves and its sister regiment, the 3rd Pennsylvania Reserves, did take part in the campaign to destroy the Virginia & Tennessee Railroad in the spring of 1864. Although they were bloodied again at the costly victory at Cloyd's Mountain in May 1864, the campaign was ultimately successful. Both Pennsylvania regiments were ordered home on May 30. Finally, on June 17, 1864, the 4th Pennsylvania Reserves was mustered out at Philadelphia. The veterans who had reenlisted and recruits were transferred to the 54th Pennsylvania Infantry.[46]

Although the 4th Pennsylvania Reserves was commanded by Major John Nyce during the Maryland Campaign, while its colonel, Albert J. Magilton, commanded the brigade, the reports for the 4th Pennsylvania Reserves were written by Captain Thomas F.B. Tapper of Company G. This is due to Major Nyce being wounded at the Battle of Antietam and being appointed colonel of the 174th Pennsylvania Infantry in November. Captain Tapper wrote of the regiment in his report, "[M]arched on the Hagerstown turnpike until it reached the base of the South Mountains. Here the regiment was marched on a road leading to the right about two miles, and formed in line of battle facing the mountains. The regiment was then ordered to advance up the mountain. At the foot of the mountain we engaged the enemy, but the regiment advanced steadily and drove the enemy over the mountain, and took up a position near the summit, and slept on our arms for the night."[47]

Colonel Magilton's Brigade report is very similar in its description of the fighting.[48] At South Mountain, the 4th Pennsylvania Reserves reported losses of five enlisted men killed, twenty-two wounded and no missing, for a total of twenty-seven.[49]

Sergeant Isaiah Thropp Jr. mustered into Company K of the 4th Pennsylvania Reserves on June 6, 1861, for three years of service. He was thirty-one years old at the time of his enlistment. Isaiah immediately got sick and is shown in a hospital during September/October 1861. There is also a note that he owed the sutler one dollar, for reasons unstated. On November 26, 1861, Corporal Thropp was detached to serve as a clerk at division headquarters. Isaiah remained a clerk until August 1, 1862, when he was appointed ordnance sergeant and returned to the 4th Pennsylvania Reserves. For the rest of his enlistment, Sergeant Thropp was present until his muster out. During the July/August 1863 period, there is a note in his

Sergeant Isaiah Thropp Jr., 4th Pennsylvania
Reserves. The reverse of Thropp's image is
blank.

service records that he was due the difference in pay for a sergeant versus
a lieutenant for the period from August 1, 1862, to January 1863. It is not
clear what the meaning of this note is. Was Isaiah being paid as a lieutenant
while still a sergeant? He is never shown as being a lieutenant, and there
is no record of a promotion to that rank. He could have been an acting
lieutenant during this period, but again his records do not specify.

Regardless, Isaiah mustered out on June 17, 1864, having last been paid
on December 31, 1863.[50] Thropp's pension card shows that he filed for a
pension on July 24, 1890, and passed away on March 3, 1921, at the age of
ninety-one. Later, his widow also received a pension.[51]

WHILE THE IMAGE OF Isaiah Thropp is very limited, there are still several
details that can be determined. First, the back of the image is completely
blank, and there is no indication of who the photographer was or where it
was taken. This was common in CDVs up through about 1861, after which
the demand for images, due to the war, led to increasingly elaborate or
detailed advertisements on the backs of images. Although some independent
photographers may still have been using blanks at this time, it was becoming

much rarer. In addition, this CDV has been pasted onto a card with a double line border, which became common in 1863. The lack of a revenue tax stamp also suggests an earlier date.[52] With the amount of time spent in Washington by the 4th Pennsylvania Reserves, it seems likely that this was done almost immediately after Isaiah Thropp's enlistment in 1861 or shortly after the regiment transferred to Washington in early 1863.

Isaiah Thropp chose a bust shot for his image. Although only the neck and the slope of the shoulders are visible, the short, standing and clasped collar gives his coat away as a frock. There was significant variation in frock coats during the Civil War, and this particular coat lacks the colored piping used to identify branch of service.[53] The first of what would be nine large Federal eagle buttons can just be seen under his beard. Thropp's beard is neatly trimmed, and his hair has been oiled and combed for the image. This image was also likely a gift, as Isaiah has signed the bottom, "Yours truly Isaiah I Thropp."

36TH PENNSYLVANIA INFANTRY / 7TH PENNSYLVANIA RESERVES

The 7th Pennsylvania Reserves was organized on June 26, 1861, at Camp Wayne, West Chester, Pennsylvania. The regiment was ordered to Washington on July 21, 1861 and mustered into the service of the United States on July 27 for a three-year enlistment. On August 2, the 7th Pennsylvania Reserves marched to Tennallytown and was assigned to the 2nd Brigade under Brigadier General George G. Meade.[54] The following year, the 7th Pennsylvania Reserves and its comrades in the 2nd Brigade took part in the fighting on the Peninsula, as well as at Second Bull Run, in the Maryland Campaign and at Fredericksburg. Following the Mud March in the early winter of 1863, the soldiers of the 2nd Brigade were sent to the Washington defenses to recuperate. They remained there throughout 1863 but rejoined the Army of the Potomac in time for the Overland Campaign in the spring of 1864.

The 7th Pennsylvania Reserves, now part of the V Corps, fought at the Battle of the Wilderness at the opening of the Overland Campaign. It was during this action that a large detachment of the regiment was cut off and captured. The remaining portion of the regiment stayed with the army until June, at which point the regiment was ordered home at the end of its enlistment. The veterans who had reenlisted and recruits were then transferred to the 190th Pennsylvania Infantry, and the regiment was mustered out in Philadelphia on June 16, 1864.[55]

Major Chauncey Lyman's report of the actions of the 7th Pennsylvania Reserves at South Mountain stated, "I have the honor to report that on the 14th of September, 1862, the Seventh Regiment, under command of Colonel (Henry C.) Bolinger, marched from camp near Frederick City to South Mountain, and was engaged with the brigade in that battle. Our loss was inconsiderable, except that Colonel Bolinger was seriously wounded during the action, and the command of the regiment devolved upon myself."[56]

Although Major Lyman recorded that Colonel Henry Bolinger had been wounded during the fighting at Frosttown Gap on South Mountain, this was not taken into account for the final casualty figures. The 7th Pennsylvania Reserves reported losses of five enlisted killed, seven enlisted wounded and no missing, for a total of twelve on September 14.[57]

One of those uninjured on September 14 was Sergeant Ernest Snowwhite. Born in Hamburg, Germany, Ernest Snowwhite immigrated to the United States in 1849. At the outbreak of war, he mustered into Company C of the 7th Pennsylvania Reserves on July 27, 1861, for three years of service. At that time, Ernest stated he was twenty-eight years old and working as distiller in Palmyra, Lebanon County, Pennsylvania. His service records show him as "not stated" through October 31, 1861, after which he was "present." Ernest entered the service as a second sergeant. During March/April 1862, he was promoted to first sergeant of his company. In July/August 1862, Ernest was shown as being assigned as the ordnance sergeant of the 7th Pennsylvania Reserves; however, there is a note that Ernest was "acting 2nd Lt. since June 30, 1862." Making it through the Battle of South Mountain on September 14, Sergeant Snowwhite was reported as "wounded in action" on September 17, 1862, at the Battle of Antietam—a gunshot wound to the right thigh. On November 10, 1862, Ernest Snowwhite was promoted to second lieutenant of Company C. Present throughout the winter of 1863, Ernest was a lieutenant commanding the company from November 1, 1862, to February 23, 1863. His promotion to first lieutenant occurred on July 20, 1863. During November/December 1863, Ernest was due pay for commanding the company as of December 8, 1863. The next event in his service records was that Ernest received a ten-day leave, and on January 14, 1864, he was assigned to special duty, although this was not specified. Lieutenant Snowwhite was reported "Missing in Action" on either May 5 or 6, 1864, during the Battle of the Wilderness.[58] Captured during the battle, Ernest likely spent time in several prisoner of war camps, but eventually he was reported as confined in Camp Asylum on the outskirts of Columbia, South Carolina. This was a camp specifically for Union officers and was on the grounds of the Columbia Insane Asylum. The camp was evacuated in February 1865 with the approach of Major General William T. Sherman's forces.[59] Ernest was paroled in North Carolina on March 1, 1865, and mustered out on March 12. Lieutenant Snowwhite was brevetted to captain for his gallant conduct at the Battle of the Wilderness as of March 13, 1865.[60] Two months later, Ernest Snowwhite applied for and received a passport on May 15, 1865.[61]

After his time in the service, Ernest Snowwhite kept up an interest in the military. The Lebanon Cadets was organized on September 16, 1869, and Ernest was elected captain of the militia company.[62] By the 1870s, he was advertising his skills as a bookbinder and salesman in the Lebanon, Pennsylvania newspapers. The following decade, he moved to Dayton, Ohio, and was working as a bookbinder.[63]

Ernest Snowwhite filed for a pension on April 7, 1877.[64] In 1892, he was listed as receiving a pension from the State of Ohio as well.[65] At that time, Ernest was living in the Soldiers Home in Dayton, Ohio, where he passed away in 1902. At the time of his passing, he had one relative listed as next of kin, William T. Schneeweiss, which means "Snowwhite" in German. Ernest Snowwhite is buried at Dayton National Cemetery, Section M, Row 23, Grave 26.[66]

THIS IMAGE WAS LIKELY taken after the 7th Pennsylvania Reserves mustered out and Ernest Snowwhite was on his way home. Taken in Reading, Pennsylvania, at the Saylor's New Photography Gallery, this is an excellent example of a late war CDV. The two-cent tax stamp puts this image sometime after August 1864 and indicates that the image cost less than twenty-five cents. In addition, the decorative photographer's advertisement on the back is seen more on mid- to late war images.[67]

The Sayler's New Photography Gallery provided a tasseled chair for Ernest Snowwhite to sit on for this image, giving a clear view of the majority of his uniform. While his footwear cannot be seen, his trousers appear to be a pair of simple sky blue kersey wool trousers that lack the eighth-of-an-inch dark-blue piping along the seam. His officer's frock coat has all nine of the large Federal eagle buttons visible, as well as the three cuff buttons of his right sleeve. Around Ernest's waist is an officer's sword belt. The belt,

Left: Sergeant Ernest Snowwhite, 7th Pennsylvania Reserves. *Right*: Back of Snowwhite's image.

according to regulations, was to be plain black leather, between 1.5 and 2 inches wide, with two saber slings about an inch wide and with a rectangular brass plate. In this case, the saber slings would be along Ernest Snowwhite's opposite hip and are not visible. His brass sword belt plate is an excellent example of a variation on the 2-inch-wide Model 1851 plate. In this case, it does not appear that the eagle or scroll of the Arms of the United States has been picked out in silver, as stated in the regulations.[68] Instead, this may be a stamped solid brass plate, although the scrollwork and motto of the United States, "E PLURIBUS UNUM," are still present.[69]

Other symbols of rank include Ernest Snowwhite's shoulder boards, with their gold embroidered edges and a single gold bar within the board to indicate a first lieutenant. Ernest is also holding his hat; sometimes referred to as a slouch hat, these comfortable black felt hats were very popular with officers. In this case, Ernest has included an officer's hat cord, which can just be seen around the crown. This cord was black and gold with acorn finials, one of which can be seen near his knee.[70]

Finally, Ernest Snowwhite has taken the time to neatly trim his mustache and shape his beard. He has also combed his dark hair back, likely having applied some sort of pomade to help hold it in place and give his hair a slight shine.

37ᵀᴴ PENNSYLVANIA INFANTRY / 8ᵀᴴ PENNSYLVANIA RESERVES

The 37th Pennsylvania Infantry, known as the 8th Pennsylvania Reserves, was organized at Camp Wright on the Allegheny River and mustered into United States service for three years on June 28, 1861. The regiment rendezvoused at Camp Wilkins, near Pittsburg, until ordered to Washington on July 20. As with the rest of the Pennsylvania Reserves, the 8th Pennsylvania Reserves was ordered to Tennallytown on August 2, 1861; there it was assigned to the 1st Brigade, Pennsylvania Reserves, under Brigadier General John F. Reynolds. The fall and winter of 1861 saw extensive training and marching for the men of the 1st Brigade. The following spring, in 1862, the brigade was assigned to the I Corps, Army of the Potomac, and did not take part in the initial movement to the Peninsula. By early summer, however, that had changed.[71] The 8th Pennsylvania Reserves fought through the Seven Days and later the Second Battle of Bull Run, the Maryland Campaign and Fredericksburg before going into winter quarters. Along with the rest of its brigade, the 8th Pennsylvania Reserves was ordered to the defenses of Washington to recuperate during the winter of 1863. It remained there for more than a year, rejoining the Army of the Potomac in April 1864. That spring, the 8th Pennsylvania Reserves fought in the Battle of the Wilderness and in the subsequent actions of the Overland Campaign until May 17. Ordered home at the end of its enlistment, the 8th Pennsylvania Reserves mustered out at Pittsburg on May 24, 1864. Those veterans who had reenlisted and the recruits were transferred to the 191st Pennsylvania Infantry.[72]

In his report of the actions of the 8th Pennsylvania Reserves at South Mountain, Major Silas M. Baily wrote, "The Third Brigade having been sent toward the right, the Eighth Regiment formed the extreme left of the division. The order to advance soon passed along the line, which the men responded to in fine style, and were soon engaged with the enemy on the mountain side, whom they drove at every point, and about dark had the satisfaction of seeing the last of them pushed over the brow of the hill in full retreat, leaving their dead and wounded in our hands."[73]

The 8th Pennsylvania Reserves had been transferred to the 2nd Brigade of the Pennsylvania Reserves Division, commanded by Colonel Albert Magilton, earlier in 1862. It was with this small brigade that the 8th Pennsylvania Reserves had the dubious honor of sustaining the most casualties of any of the three regiments in the 2nd Brigade at South Mountain, with one officer and fourteen enlisted men killed, one officer and thirty-three men wounded and one man missing, for a total of fifty casualties, more than the other regiments combined. The 8th Pennsylvania Reserves had nearly the highest casualty rate of any regiment in the entire division on September 14, 1862.[74]

Leading his men up South Mountain and through Frosttown Gap was Captain John M. Kent of Company I. John Kent had mustered into Company I of the 8th Pennsylvania Reserves for three years on July 29, 1861. He stated that he was twenty-five and was mustered in as a first lieutenant. John was "present" on the August 31 muster roll, but as was common for the rest of 1861, his status was "not stated." On November 21, 1861, John was appointed adjutant or the administrative assistant to commander of the 8th Pennsylvania Reserves. The following year, he was elected captain of Company I on June 16, 1862. John's status was again "not stated" for July/ August; however, he was listed as "present" for September/October during the Maryland Campaign. The next event in his service records was his being "wounded in action" on December 13, 1862, at the Battle of Fredericksburg. He was sent to a hospital, which was not identified, nor was the wound described on the casualty page of his records. Another note in the March/ April 1863 report states that John was "due pay for respon[sibility] for arms and clothing for month of January and February 1863." On July 26, 1863, Captain Kent was detached to the Provost Marshal's Office in Alexandria, Virginia. He returned to the 8th Pennsylvania Reserves during January/ February 1864. At that time, John was due an extra ten dollars per month from October 31, 1863, for again taking responsibility for the arms and clothing of his company. Once back with the Army of the Potomac, Captain Kent was wounded a second time, this time at the Battle of the Wilderness in early May 1864. No description of the wound was given, but it may have been slight, as John Kent was present with his company until his muster out with the rest of the 8th Pennsylvania Reserves on May 24, 1864. He had last been paid on February 29, 1864.[75]

John Kent was not done with his service, however, as he reenlisted on September 8, 1864, as captain of Battery K, 5th Pennsylvania Heavy Artillery. He served until June 30, 1865, as part of the mobile defense of Washington,

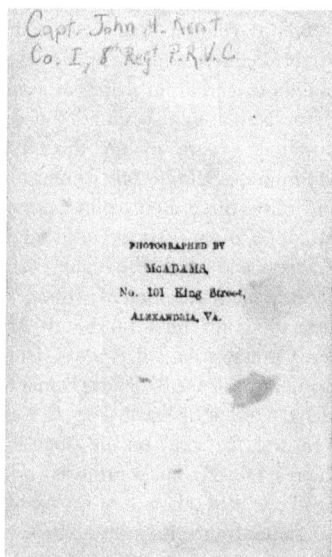

Left: Captain John M. Kent, 8th Pennsylvania Reserves. *Right*: Back of Kent's image.

D.C., and filed for a pension on August 4, 1865.[76] Continuing his service to his state, Kent later served as the captain of Company K, 10th Pennsylvania National Guard, during the Pennsylvania Railroad Strike of 1877.[77] John Kent passed away on July 2, 1891, at the age of fifty-five. He was buried at Waynesburg, Pennsylvania's Green Mount Cemetery on July 4, 1891, in Section D, Lot 40.[78]

AS THIS IMAGE WAS taken at the McAdams gallery in Alexandria, Virginia, Captain John Kent was likely photographed in the summer of 1863. By that point, the 8th Pennsylvania Reserves had been shifted into the Washington Defenses and John Kent was on detached duty in the Provost Marshal's Office in Alexandria. The image itself has a simple stamped advertisement on the back, and a previous collector has made note of Kent's name, rank and regiment.

The image is a bust view, only showing the upper half of John Kent's torso. However, the details that are available make it clear that he is wearing an officer's frock coat. The four large, closely spaced Federal eagle buttons, along with the short, standing, possibly velvet collar, give this away. As for the buttons themselves, four of the nine are visible and are quite clear in this image. As Kent was an officer, these buttons should have the infantry "I" on the shield and eagle design, as opposed to a blank shield for the enlisted men.[79] Beneath the frock, which is only buttoned at the top, is Kent's officer's vest, with two of its small eagle buttons visible. On his shoulders are rather large gold embroidered shoulder boards, with two gold bars in the interior to signify his rank. Finally, he is wearing a new paper collar for this image, and the knot of a small black cravat can just be seen at the base of the neck. John Kent has a thick, short beard just under his chin that he has trimmed, and he has combed back and oiled his hair as a finishing touch.

THE FIGHTING AT FROSTTOWN Gap began much later than the fighting elsewhere on South Mountain. As such, this portion of the Battle of South Mountain continued to rage until well after sunset. By nightfall, the gap and the high ground around it were in Union hands. The Federal troops who had attacked up South Mountain at Frosttown Gap encountered some of the most difficult terrain imaginable. In the waning light that Sunday, they had met and forced back the dogged defense of Brigadier General Robert Rodes and his brigade of Alabama regiments before camping that night on the field among the dead and wounded.

Of the six men mentioned here, none was wounded at South Mountain. Three days later, however, both Lieutenant Jamison and Corporal Rohm were reported wounded at the Battle of Antietam. Captain Kent was wounded twice after the Battle of South Mountain—once at Fredericksburg in December 1862 and again in the Wilderness in May 1864. Sergeant Russell paid the ultimate price for his service and was mortally wounded in the Battle of the Wilderness, while Lieutenant Snowwhite was captured there. Only Ordnance Sergeant Thropp survived the war unscathed or without being captured. Thropp, along with Jamison and Snowwhite, lived into the twentieth century; sadly, neither Rohm nor Kent did, both dying relatively young. The next day, September 15, 1862, found these men on the move yet again, this time headed for the bloodiest day in American history on the banks of a Western Maryland creek called Antietam.

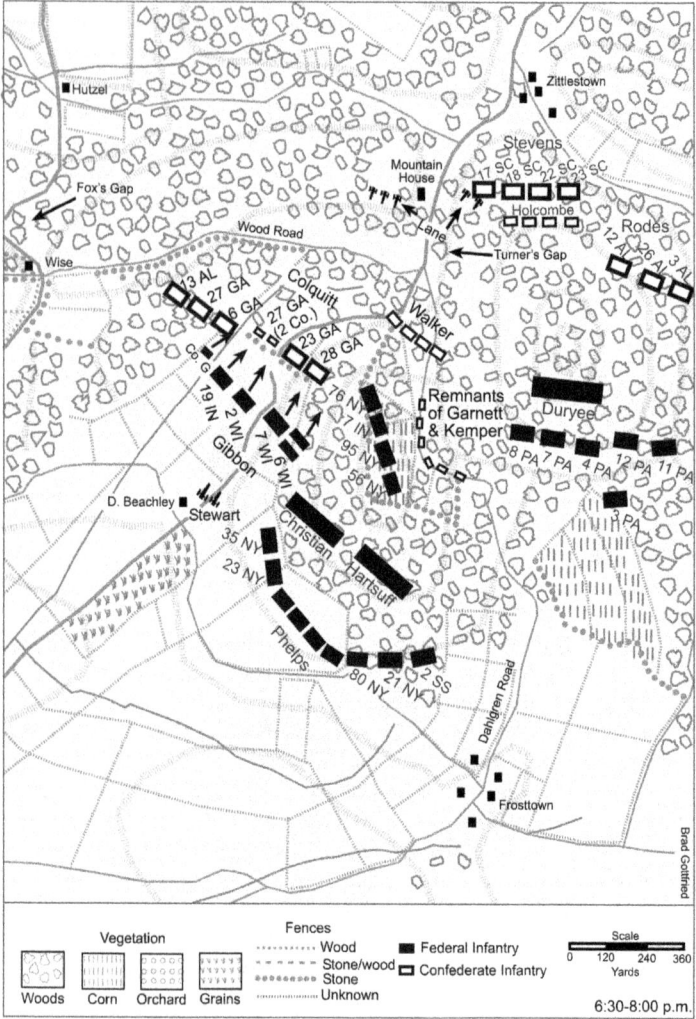

South Mountain—Turner's Gap, 6:30 p.m.–8:00 p.m. *Map provided by Dr. Bradley Gottfried.*

Chapter 2

TURNER'S GAP

As the I Corps soldiers of Brigadier General George Meade's Division were engaged farther to the north at Frosttown Gap, an additional attack was ordered to advance on Turner's Gap following the National Road around 5:00 p.m. Approaching Turner's Gap between 6:30 p.m. and 8:00 p.m. was the division of Brigadier General John P. Hatch. During the intense fighting up South Mountain at Turner's Gap, General Hatch was wounded in the leg. As such, command of the division fell to Brigadier General Abner Doubleday, who stated in his after-action report:

> [T]his division left Monocacy at 6 a.m. September 14, and arrived at the Catoctin about 12:30 p.m. Here the column halted until 2:30 p.m., when Brigadier General Hatch assumed command.... The enemy's position was on the summit of South Mountain. To avoid the fire of his batteries, the division now diverged from the main road and struck off into a by-road to the right, which led to a stone church at the foot of the mountain, where we found General Hooker and his staff...
>
> On reaching a road part way up the mountain, and parallel to its summit, each brigade deployed in turn and advanced in line of battle.... General Patrick rode to the front with his skirmishers, drew the fire of the enemy, and developed their position. They lay behind a fence on the summit running north and south, fronted by a woods and backed by a corn-field, full of rocky ledges. Colonel Phelps now ordered his men to advance, and General Hatch rode through the lines, pressing them

forward. They went in with a cheer, poured in a deadly fire, and drove
the enemy from his position behind the fence, after a short and desperate
conflict, and took post some yards beyond.
Here General Hatch was wounded and turned over the command to me.[80]

As General Hatch's Division advanced up South Mountain, to its right was the left end of General Meade's Division. On the extreme left of Hatch's Division was Brigadier General John Gibbon's Brigade of midwestern troops, who had already begun build a reputation for themselves. In this brigade was the 2nd Wisconsin Infantry. Roughly to the right and slightly farther north was the 76th New York Infantry of Brigadier General Abner Doubleday's Brigade. Farther to the rear was the 23rd New York Infantry of Colonel Walter Phelps's Brigade. To the right and forward of the 23rd New York was the 83rd New York Infantry of Brigadier General George Hartsuff's Brigade. Finally, to the far right was Brigadier General Abram Duryee's Brigade, which contained the 97th New York Infantry and the 105th New York Infantry. They were positioned in front of the left end of Meade's Division. The positions of these units are shown on the map.

2ND WISCONSIN INFANTRY

As one of the first three-year regiments to be raised for the Civil War, the 2nd Wisconsin Infantry was organized in May 1861 and was mustered into service on June 11 with a strength of 1,048 officers and men. The regiment left the state on June 20 and arrived at the nation's capital five days later. Initially assigned to the brigade of Colonel William T. Sherman, along with three New York regiments, the Badger State men fought at the First Battle of Bull Run.[81]

By late 1861, the 2nd Wisconsin had been reassigned to a brigade made up of all midwestern regiments, the only such organization in the Army of the Potomac. At the time, the brigade included the 6th and 7th Wisconsin Infantry, as well as the 19th Indiana Infantry. On May 7, 1862, Brigadier General John Gibbon, a strict disciplinarian, was assigned to command the rambunctious midwestern troops.[82] He soon had them drilling hard and uniformly equipped in the uniform of the American army prior to the war. Due to its use of the regulation Model 1858 black Hardee hat, the brigade was soon known as the "Black Hats" or the "Black Hat Brigade."[83]

The brigade earned a reputation for hard fighting during the late summer and fall of 1862. During that period, it was heavily engaged during the opening of the Second Battle of Bull Run, fought up South Mountain and in the Cornfield at Antietam during the Maryland Campaign and ended the year with the Battle of Fredericksburg. By this point, the brigade had been reinforced by the 24th Michigan Infantry and had a new nickname, earned during the Maryland Campaign: the "Iron Brigade."[84]

The men of the Iron Brigade were heavily engaged during the Gettysburg Campaign in 1863 and the Overland Campaign in the spring of 1864. These campaigns so reduced the 2nd Wisconsin in numbers that it was permanently detached from the brigade on May 11, 1864. For the next month, the 2nd Wisconsin was utilized as the provost guard of the 4th Division, V Corps, until June 11, 1864. When the regiment was returned to Wisconsin, the last company mustered out of service on July 2, 1864.[85]

The commander of the 2nd Wisconsin, Colonel Lucius Fairchild, wrote the report covering the actions of the regiment at the Battle of South Mountain:

> *Soon after a large portion of Hookers corps were in line, and advancing up the mountain on the right of the turnpike. Gibbon's brigade advanced on the pike to the foot of the mountain. On arriving there, the Nineteenth Indiana Volunteers and my regiment filed into the field on the left. Companies B and E of my regiment were deployed as skirmishers, and ordered to advance, their right resting on the pike. The Nineteenth Indiana followed, with my regiment in their rear about 200 yards. By order of General Gibbon, we moved thus in double column until well within the gap. While lying down in that position, a shell from the enemy struck and exploded in the ranks of the second division of the Second Regiment, killing 4 and badly wounding 3. Soon after, I deployed my column, the skirmishers being briskly engaged, and, when the Nineteenth Indiana opened fire, I moved forward to their right, the right of my regiment resting on the turnpike, and opened fire. After expending some 20 rounds of ammunition, I discovered the enemy had entirely disappeared from our front. Then I ordered the men to fire by the right-oblique, on a line of the enemy who were firing on the Seventh Wisconsin. After a short time I ceased firing, and, the better to get at the enemy, changed direction with the right wing of my regiment. In that position good execution was done until their ammunition was all expended, when they were withdrawn to the line, and the left wing took their place. After the left wing had expended their ammunition and had*

been withdrawn, the Nineteenth took the same position, by wings. All were then ordered to lie down. The fire from the enemy ceased and all was quiet. I ordered Company A to deploy as skirmishers to the extreme left of the Nineteenth Indiana, and sent a few men to the front a short distance, to prevent a surprise. Thus we lay until nearly midnight, when part of General Gorman's brigade took our ground, while we fell back a short distance for ammunition. The action was not resumed after my regiment left the front line. Fortunately the Second suffered lightly in comparison with other regiments of the brigade.[86]

The 2nd Wisconsin was very fortunate at South Mountain when compared with the rest of Gibbon's Brigade. The regiment reported losses of one officer and five enlisted killed, one officer and eighteen enlisted wounded and one man missing, for a total of twenty-six.[87]

Lucius Fairchild was born in Franklin Mills, Ohio, on December 27, 1831. The Fairchild family moved in 1846 to Wisconsin, where Lucius became well known with many friends. After an unimpressive run at the Prairieville Academy, Lucius Fairchild went west at age seventeen to participate in the gold rush. He returned to Wisconsin in 1855, having found some financial success in California. Prior to the war, in 1858, Lucius joined a volunteer militia company known as the "Governor's Guard" and had become the company captain by 1861. At the outbreak of hostilities, the Governor's Guard was mustered in as Company K, 1st Wisconsin Volunteers, a three-month regiment. After taking part in the skirmish at Falling Waters, Virginia, the regiment was mustered out on August 5, 1861. Captain Fairchild was promoted to the rank of lieutenant in the regular army, but prior to joining the regular service, he was appointed lieutenant colonel of the 2nd Wisconsin Infantry and joined his new regiment in Washington. One year later, he commanded the consolidated 2nd and 7th Wisconsin regiments at the Second Battle of Bull Run. Following the battle, he was promoted to colonel, to date from August 30, 1862, and led the 2nd Wisconsin on September 14, when it attacked and carried Turner's Gap during the Battle of South Mountain. Three days later, on September 17, although sick, Fairchild was lifted onto his horse and commanded his regiment through the Battle of Antietam. At the Battle of Fredericksburg on December 13, 1862, he won a special commendation from Brigadier General Solomon Meredith for his handling of the 2nd Wisconsin during the battle. In the spring of 1863, he rendered important service at Chancellorsville and at Gettysburg that

Left: Colonel Lucius Fairchild, 2nd Wisconsin Infantry. *Right*: Back of Fairchild's image.

summer led a charge up Seminary Hill, where he lost his left arm. Colonel Fairchild was captured when Confederate forces took Gettysburg but was immediately paroled due to his recent amputation. While recovering from his wound, he was commissioned brigadier general of volunteers on October 19, 1863, and on November 2, 1863, he was mustered out of the service.[88] Lucius Fairchild served in several government positions and was active in both the Grand Army of the Republic and the Military Order of the Loyal Legion of the United States veterans organizations after the war.[89] General Fairchild died in Madison, Wisconsin, on May 23, 1896, of Bright's disease. He was sixty-five years old at the time and was buried at Forest Hill Cemetery, Section 32, Lot 14, 15, 18 and 17 SW.[90]

THIS BUST VIEW OF Lucius Fairchild was taken at Mathew Brady's National Portrait Gallery. The image was likely taken in October 1863, after his promotion to brigadier general but prior to his resignation from the service in November to take the position of Wisconsin's secretary of state. Fairchild is wearing an officer's frock, likely his colonel's frock, as it appears to have the double rows of seven evenly spaced buttons, three of each row being visible, as opposed to the two rows of eight buttons, which would have been closely paired together per a brigadier general's coat.[91] His left shoulder board is prominent in this photo, with its dark-blue or black interior and a single gold star for a brigadier. Fairchild appears to have stuck with regulations, as the gold embroidery making up the border of the shoulder board is only 0.25 inches wide. Officers were allowed to have wider borders if they wished, up to 0.375 inches wide.[92] Lucius Fairchild is wearing a new paper collar for this image that can just be seen at his coat collar. He has also neatly trimmed his full beard and combed his hair back from his high forehead.[93]

76TH NEW YORK INFANTRY

The 76th New York, known as the "Cortland Regiment," was recruited primarily in Cortland and Otsego Counties of New York. However, due to difficulty raising an entire regiment from the county, as well as internal strife in the command structure, meant that the 76th New York did not move to Albany, the state capital, until December 18, 1861. Otsego County was also trying to raise its own regiment but found its recruiting coming up short as well. The companies of the proposed Otsego regiment were ordered to Albany on January 8, 1862. There, three of the Otsego companies were assigned to the 76th New York. Now at full strength, the 76th New York mustered into the service of the United States at Albany on January 16, 1862, for three years.[94]

Upon its arrival in Washington, the 76th New York was assigned to the 3rd Brigade of Brigadier General Silas Casey's Division and served in the vicinity of Washington throughout the winter and into the summer of 1862 before being ordered to join Major General John Pope's Union Army of Virginia in August. Following the fighting at Second Bull Run, the 76th New York took part in the Maryland Campaign, the fighting in the Loudoun Valley and the Battle of Fredericksburg. The regiment was also at Gettysburg in the summer of 1863. In the winter of 1864, the 76th New York was transferred to the V Corps and fought with it through the Overland Campaign and the opening of the Siege of Petersburg. The 76th New York mustered out by companies from July 1, 1864, through January 1, 1865. After this, the reenlisted veterans and recruits were transferred to the 147[95] New York Infantry. The regiment lost during its term of service 175 men by death from wounds and 166 by death from accident, imprisonment or disease, of whom 56 died in imprisonment.[95]

During the Battle of South Mountain, Colonel William Wainwright was ordered to take command of Brigadier General Abner Doubleday's Brigade when Doubleday took over the division for the wounded Brigadier General John P. Hatch. Wainwright was, in turn, wounded in the arm and had his horse killed beneath him. Though out of action, he was still able to write his report describing the actions of the 76th New York at the battle:

> [T]*he Seventy-sixth New York Volunteers passed through a line of troops under the command of General Patrick. The regiment formed with perfect steadiness on the extreme left. They were well in hand during the whole engagement, always obeyed the orders to fire and to cease firing readily, and although not many cartridges were expended, the repulse of an attempt to turn our left, which, in conjunction with the left wing of the Seventh Indiana Regiment, was brilliantly accomplished, and the orderly manner in which they afterward passed the line of troops coming up to relieve them, showed that they are fast becoming veteran soldiers.*
>
> *I would again (as in a note sent yesterday afternoon by Surgeon Metcalfe) call the general's attention to the weakened state of the regiment. They went into action on this occasion with only forty files. Their loss was, so far as ascertained, 2 killed and 13 wounded—of the latter, 2 mortally. I doubt whether they can now furnish more than thirty files, commanded by four lieutenants, in any line of battle that may be called for at present…*
>
> *Sergeant Stamp, just promoted for good conduct in a former battle, was shot through the head while gallantly carrying the national colors.*
>
> *Owing to a wound in the arm received during the action, I am unable to join the regiment. First Lieutenant Crandall is next in command.*[96]

At South Mountain, the 76th New York reported losses of two enlisted men killed, one officer and seventeen enlisted wounded and none missing, for a total loss of twenty men.[97]

William Pratt Wainwright was born on June 10, 1818, in New York City. He had a good education growing up and graduated from the University of the City of New York before beginning the study of medicine. Medicine, however, did not appeal to him, and he traveled to Europe, primarily for military studies. He spent time in Berlin, becoming fluent in German, before returning to the United States and working with the militia of Dutchess County, New York.[98]

At the outbreak of the war, William was forty-three years old and was asked to accept the position of major in the 29th New York Infantry. The 29th New York was primarily of German ancestry, and Wainwright's knowledge of the language, as well as his previous training, proved beneficial. On June 3, 1862, he accepted a promotion to colonel and command of the 76th New York Infantry. William's service records for the 76th New York show that he assumed command on July 2, 1862, and was "present" until June 1863. On September 14, 1862, William was wounded in the arm at the Battle of South Mountain; unfortunately, the casualty report in his records does not give further details. On November 8, 1862, William returned from sick leave and assumed command on November 15, 1862. There is a note in his records that during March/April 1863, William "employed one soldier as private servant." On June 16, 1863, William went on a twenty-day furlough based on a surgeon certificate. William Wainwright was honorably discharged on June 25, 1863, to accept the appointment of provost marshal for Washington. William was brevetted brigadier general for faithful and meritorious service on March 13, 1865, but he declined the promotion on July 20, 1868.[99] On June 23, 1890, William filed for a pension. Although no date of death is listed with his pension information,[100] elsewhere his date of death is given as October 17, 1895, in New York City.[101] William Wainwright was laid to rest at what is today the Rhinebeck Association Cemetery in Rhinebeck, New York, on October 19, 1895.[102]

This full standing image of William Wainwright was most likely taken in the early summer of 1862, just after his promotion to colonel of the 76th New York Infantry. Taken at the Addis Gallery in Washington, this particular CDV appears to have been a gift, as it is signed not only on the front with "Col. Wainwright 76th Regt N.Y.V." but also on the back with "William P." In addition, someone has taken the time to write "belongs to C___ Smith" on the back of the image.

The Addis Gallery provided a carpeted gallery space, as well as a large decorative drape with tasseled cord. This was a common decoration for the period, but it was also likely being used to hide the brace helping to keep William Wainwright still for the image. The bunching of the drape

Left: Colonel William Pratt Wainwright, 76th New York Infantry. *Right*: Back of Wainwright's image.

behind Wainwright's feet suggests that it was being used to cover the legs of said brace.

On the colonel's feet are nondescript leather shoes, the smooth side being out indicating a higher quality. This could be a half-boot, also known as an ankle boot (worn with the trousers on the outside), as many officers preferred the lighter shoe. Colonel Wainwright's dark-blue trousers are indicative of officer's trousers prior to General Orders No. 108 and the introduction of the light-blue, kersey wool trousers.[103] The eighth-of-an-inch sky blue piping used by infantry officers can just be seen running up the seam of his left leg.[104]

Starting just above the knees is William Wainwright's frock coat. His officer's frock is clearly defined by the double row of seven large eagle buttons, six buttons being visible on each row.[105] The seventh button for each row is covered by Wainwright's belt. As he was an officer, these buttons likely have the branch of service indicated on them with a letter, in this case an "I" for the infantry.[106] Three additional buttons can be seen along the left cuff;

these small eagle buttons are also an indication of an officer's frock. Finally, Colonel Wainwright is wearing his shoulder boards. Though washed out in this image, these gold embroidered symbols of rank would have a spread eagle made of silver thread embroidered in the center of the board on a field of sky or light blue for the infantry.[107]

Just as prominent in this photo, but not as often recognized as a symbol of rank, is Colonel Wainwright's belt and sword. It is difficult to tell, but it does not appear that Wainwright is wearing a sash under his sword belt, just the belt itself. The belt is black leather, no more than two inches wide, with two saber slings to attach the officer's scabbard to the belt. The slings can be seen coming off the belt just above Wainwright's left hand and off the second loop on his scabbard. This particular sword belt is an example of the regulation belt, which varied from contractor to contractor. The belt plate in this image has been washed out by the flash, but it would have been a solid brass plate with a raised rim, two inches wide and two and three-quarter inches long. The Federal eagle, with wings spread, was featured on these belt plates for officers and noncommissioned officers alike. The eagle was framed with laurels that were often, but not always, silver and attached separately. Finally, above the eagle waves a banner inscribed with the motto of the nation, "E PLURIBUS UNUM," usually picked out in silver.[108]

As for the sword itself, with it being sheathed at Colonel William Wainwright's side, it is difficult to tell with certainty the type of blade. However, it is likely a variation of the 1850 field officer's sword prescribed in regulations—the half basket guard is a good indicator of this. Wainwright is resting his left hand on the pommel of his sword, with his fingers wrapping around the guard. The sword knot strap of gold lace with a gold bullion knot is held between his fingers and falls in front of the scabbard.[109] The scabbard itself is bright iron with brass fixtures, the first being the throat located under the guard. Both this and the middle band have suspension rings for the saber slings attached to the belt. The long finial at the end of the scabbard is called the drag and protects the tip of the scabbard from dragging on the ground.[110]

Finally, it is difficult to make out in this image, but Colonel Wainwright is holding his forage cap in his right hand. The dark-blue cap blends into the decorative drape behind Wainwright, but the short leather bill has caught some of the flash. This crescent-shaped bill gives the forage cap away as a "McDowell," a variation of the model 1858 forage cap and popularized by Major General Irvin McDowell.[111] The colonel does not appear to be wearing a cravat for this image, but rather stands bareheaded and looking directly at the camera. This was at the beginning of his time with the 76th New York, but he has already seen action, which is portrayed in his eyes.

23RD NEW YORK INFANTRY

One of New York State's two-year regiments, the 23rd New York Infantry was composed of three companies from Steuben County, two from Tioga, two from Chemung, one from Alleghany, one from Cortland and one from Schuyler and was known as the "Southern Tier Regiment" due to it being raised entirely from counties in New York State's Southern Tier region. The 23rd New York was mustered into United States service at Elmira, New York, on July 2, 1861, and left the state for Washington on July 5. Once in Washington, the 23rd New York was assigned to the defense of the capital city and remained there until assigned to the Army of Virginia in June 1862. During Major General John Pope's campaign, the 23rd New York fought at Second Bull Run and Chantilly before falling back toward Washington once more.[112]

In September 1862, the 23rd New York was reassigned to the I Corps, Army of the Potomac, and fought at South Mountain and Antietam. The final battle of the 23rd New York was fought in December 1862 at Fredericksburg. After the Union defeat, the regiment fell back to Belle Plain, Virginia, and went into winter quarters. At that time, the regiment was assigned to the Provost Guard Brigade of Brigadier General Marsena Patrick. In late April 1863, the 23rd New York was ordered to Aquia Creek, Virginia, to garrison the forts there. It remained there until the end of its service. On June 26, the command was mustered out in New York City, having lost seventeen by death from wounds and fifty-five by death from other causes.[113]

At South Mountain, the 23rd New York was slightly engaged. One history stated, "Colonel Hoffman halted the 23rd about three-quarters of a mile up the hill along a farm road running parallel with the crest. Here the men left their burdensome knapsacks and after a brief rest pushed on.—By the time they arrived at the left of the mile-long Union line of battle, the evening had become 'dark as a pocket.'—The regiment fired about twelve rounds with little appreciable effect before the order to cease fire arrived from the right of the line.—The 23rd emerged from the fighting with but six men slightly wounded."[114]

Tending to those wounded men was Major William A. Madill. The son of Irish immigrants, William Madill mustered into the field and staff of the 23rd New York Infantry on May 16, 1861, at Elmira, New York, as the assistant surgeon with the rank of first lieutenant. At the time of his enlistment, he stated that he was twenty-eight years old. As was common, his status was shown as "not stated" until the January/February 1862 period, when William was listed as "present." William remained listed as such for the rest of his service in the 23rd New York. He was promoted to surgeon of the 23rd New York Infantry on August 7, 1862, following the resignation of Surgeon Seymour Churchill on June 23, 1862. As surgeon, Madill held the rank of major. William completed his two years with the 23rd New York Infantry and mustered out on May 22, 1863; he had last been paid on February 28, 1863.[115] However, William's service to the Union was not over, as he mustered into the field and staff of the 20th New York Cavalry as the regimental surgeon on July 18, 1863. William served in the 20th New York Cavalry until July 31, 1865.[116] After the war, he returned to private practice and was listed as a physician in the 1870 and 1880 censuses.[117] Dr. William Madill was fifty-five when he died on September 10, 1889, and is buried at Wysox Cemetery, Bradford County, Pennsylvania.[118]

This image of Dr. William Madill was taken at one of Mathew Brady's National Portrait Gallery locations, most likely the Washington gallery. His name and position as surgeon have been noted on the back by a collector. As Madill is a major in this photograph, the CDV was taken sometime after August 7, 1862, when William Madill was promoted in the field to surgeon and obtained that rank.[119] The 23rd New York Infantry did camp near the nation's capital following the Union defeat at Second Bull Run and then passed through Washington as the Maryland Campaign began. It is likely that this image was taken at that time.

Several items have been provided by the National Portrait Gallery to add to the picture and support Dr. William Madill during the exposure. A decorative drape partially covers the wall behind the surgeon, while a fine table provides not only a brace but also a platform for his sword. Just behind Madill, the feet of a brace can be made out, to help further steady the surgeon for the image.

A full standing image, Dr. William Madill apparently has on officer's boots or ankle boots, as they are tapering slightly toward the toe.[120] This

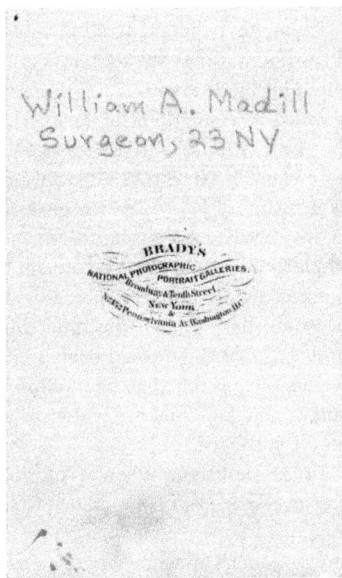

Left: Surgeon William A. Madill, 23rd New York Infantry. *Right*: Back of Madill's image.

was not out of the ordinary, as a regimental surgeon usually rode instead of marching. Madill has opted for the dark-blue officer's trousers, as he was a regimental officer; these trousers had an eighth-of-an-inch welt along the seam, in this case light blue for the infantry, which can be seen running up the left leg. Coming right to the knees of these trousers is the skirting of Dr. Madill's very large officer's frock coat. The extra length of the skirting, the full sleeves and the velvet collar are all common features of an officer's frock.[121] However, it is the two rows of seven buttons that really give it away as belonging to an officer. The buttons themselves are quite large and have a prominent ring design, making it likely that these are New York State buttons with the state seal on them.[122] Finishing off the frock are Madill's shoulder boards. They have the usual gold embroidered borders, but inside on each end is a gold oak leaf, to indicate a major. The interior color of the shoulder board is supposed to correlate to the branch of service; as a field and staff officer, the internal color of the shoulder board here is dark blue or black.[123]

Although William Madill is not wearing the green sash of the medical department, nor a sword belt over it, there is a sword on the table to his left. This blade could be a prop provided by the gallery, but he was given a sword in recognition of his service by the men in Company K of the 23rd New York Infantry. This occurred in late August 1861, around the time the 23rd New York engaged in a skirmish at Cow's Run. Described as a beautiful sword, it was given "in recognition of their appreciation of his services as Assistant-Surgeon."[124] It seems very likely that Madill would want to include this blade in his image. While the sword pictured is not a medical officer's sword, it is unlikely that the soldiers of Company K would have known the difference as listed in the regulations.[125] It is probable that they would have purchased a sword that they were used to seeing, such as the 1850 field officer's sword. The heavily decorated guard and the quillon finial are visible, as are the throat and second brass fixture on the scabbard.[126]

In Dr. Madill's right hand is his slouch hat. This comfortable black felt hat had a wide brim with a binding of black silk. Popular with both officers and men, the officer's slouch hat had a cord of black silk and gold around the crown, which can be seen in this image, along with the acorn-shaped finials that are clearly visible.[127] To finish off his appearance, Madill is wearing a new paper collar, seen peeking above the velvet collar of his frock coat. He has also neatly trimmed his beard and combed his hair. Interestingly, the image appears to have caught Dr. Madill as he was glancing up.

83RD NEW YORK INFANTRY

The 83rd New York, first known as the 9th New York State Militia, was recruited in New York City and left the state for Washington on May 27, 1861. There the regiment was mustered into United States service for a three-year term on June 8. The 83rd New York served along the Potomac River in Maryland and at Harpers Ferry throughout 1861 and into the winter of 1862. Ordered to the Union Army of Virginia in late June 1862, the 83rd New York took part in Major General John Pope's campaign and was heavily engaged at Second Bull Run. Following the reorganization of Union forces around Washington, the 83rd New York joined the I Corps and saw action throughout the Maryland and Fredericksburg Campaigns. The 83rd New York remained with the I Corps throughout 1863 and was in the thick of the fighting at Gettysburg. In March 1864, the regiment was transferred to the V Corps and fought with that command through the Overland Campaign. Following the Battle of Cold Harbor, the 83rd New York Infantry was pulled off the line due to the expiration of its term of service.[128] Mustered out in New York on June 23, 1864, the veterans who reenlisted and the new recruits were transferred to the 97th New York Infantry.

No regimental report exists for the 83rd New York at South Mountain; however, Private John W. Jaques did describe the action in his regimental history:

> [W]*e came to* SOUTH MOUNTAIN, *where the battle was being fought; taking the extreme left of the line, the Brigade advanced up the Mountain, over a steep and precipitous road, filled with brush, and small loose stones, which gave way under our feet; reaching the summit the brigade formed in line of battle. Supporting the "Pennsylvania Reserves," belonging to our Corps, who were thrown forward as skirmishers; the engagement was kept up, a long while after dark, when the firing having ceased, the Brigade fell back a short distance, on a low level plain, and supper less, laid down on our arms, tired and hungry after a fatiguing march of 12 miles.*[129]

While the 83rd New York saw only limited action at South Mountain, Brigadier General James Ricketts did mention two of its officers by name in his "List of officers and men who behaved with gallantry in the engagements of September 14–17, 1862," which was attached to his after-action report. Under the "Third Brigade," he called out Captain Joseph A. Moesch and Captain John Hendrickson of the 83rd New York Infantry.[130] Being in a supporting position at South Mountain, the 83rd New York thankfully reported very few losses. These included one enlisted man killed, one man wounded and no missing, for a total of two.[131]

Mentioned in General Ricketts report was Captain John Hendrickson, born on January 21, 1833, in Middletown, New Jersey. At the outbreak of hostilities, he enlisted for the duration of the war and was commissioned as a first lieutenant on May 27, 1861, in Company G of the 83rd New York State Infantry. As was common in the early records, his status was "not stated" from June 8, 1861, to August 31, 1861. Throughout this early period, Lieutenant Hendrickson was "present" except for a brief furlough to New York City in November 1861. By July 1, 1861, he had been promoted to captain of his company. Following the Maryland

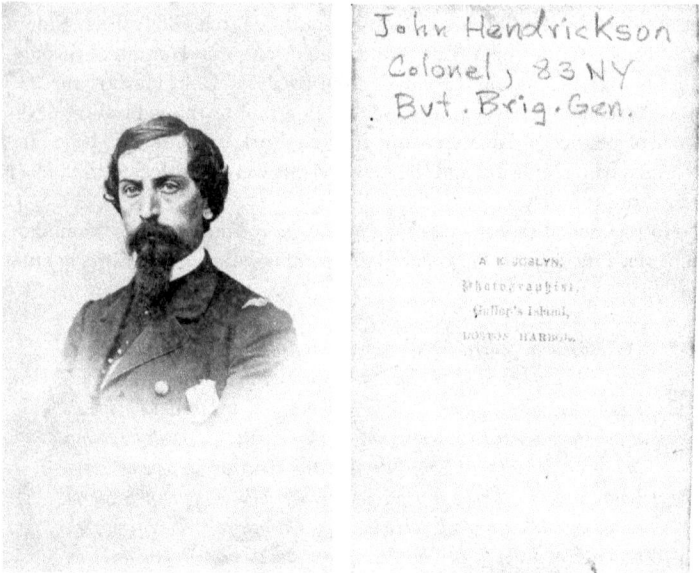

Left: Captain John Hendrickson, 83rd New York Infantry. *Right*: Back of Hendrickson's image.

Campaign in 1862, he was promoted again, this time to major, on October 10, 1862. Two months later at Fredericksburg, while commanding the 83rd New York as lieutenant colonel, Hendrickson was badly wounded on December 13, 1862, with his records stating "severely wounded in right leg, amputated." John spent some time in the Armory Square USA General Hospital in Washington after his wounding and was reported in New York in April, having likely been sent home to recover. His service records show that he was promoted to colonel on June 12, 1863, although elsewhere the date is listed as January 18, 1863. Due to the severity of his wound, however, John was absent from the 83rd New York for the rest of his service. On August 1, 1863, he resigned his commission, but later that month, on August 23, he was appointed colonel of the 9th Veteran Reserves Corps.[132]

During his time with the Veteran Reserves Corps, John Hendrickson received a brevet promotion to brigadier general on March 13, 1865.[133] He remained in the Reserves Corps until June 30, 1866, when he mustered out of the service.[134] After the war, he resided in New York City, was an active member of the veteran community and worked as a dealer in the woolen industry. John Hendrickson died suddenly on June 29, 1902, and is buried at Woodlawn Cemetery, Bronx, New York.[135]

TAKEN BY "PHOTOGRAPHIST" A.K. Joslyn on Gallop's Island in Boston Harbor, this image was made sometime after John Hendrickson's promotion to colonel. A previous collector has made note of Hendrickson's name and ranks on the back of the CDV. In the image, Hendrickson's rank insignia is clearly visible on his shoulders: a silver eagle with wings spread. However, the rank insignia are sewn directly to the coat itself; they are not attached to shoulder boards. This is sometimes referred to as a subdued rank insignia and was meant to draw less attention to officers in combat. The same is true for wearing the same greatcoats as enlisted men, lack of ornamentation on hats and dispensing with swords. While individual commands began experimenting with this idea by mid-1863, the process was formalized near the end of 1864 with General Orders No. 286.[136]

The coat that the eagles are attached to appears to be a dark-blue, double-breasted fatigue blouse. The folding collar and lapels make it clear that it is not a frock coat, while the button on the same side as a buttonhole marks it as double breasted.[137] John Hendrickson has some sort of neckerchief or perhaps a favor poking out of his breast pocket as well. The coat is open, exposing a dark-blue civilian vest. The buttons, of which seven are visible, look to be smaller than even the small Federal eagle buttons and may be rounded. At least four of the buttons are undone, exposing the white shirt underneath, likely for ventilation. The paper collar of that same shirt is prominent, standing stiffly over the coat collar. John Hendrickson has also neatly trimmed his beard and combed his hair for both his image and regulations.

97TH NEW YORK INFANTRY

Known as the Conkling Rifles, named for New York congressman Roscoe Conkling,[138] the 97th New York Infantry was recruited in Oneida and Herkimer Counties and mustered into United States service at Boonville, New York, on February 18, 1862, for three years of service. The regiment left for Washington on March 12 and was quartered at Fort Corcoran, just across the Potomac River from Georgetown, as part of Brigadier General James Wadsworth's Military District of Washington. The 97th New York later served in the Department of the Rappahannock until transferred to Major General John Pope's Army of Virginia in late June 1862. Under Pope, the regiment fought at Cedar Mountain and through the Northern Virginia Campaign, going into action along the Rappahannock River and at Second Bull Run. After this, the 97th New York was transferred to the I Corps. It remained with the I Corps through the Maryland Campaign, suffering heavily at Antietam. The 97th New York was at Fredericksburg in December 1862 but did not participate in Chancellorsville in the spring of 1863. The rest of 1863 saw heavy fighting for the regiment. Over the winter, the 97th New York reenlisted enough men to retain its formation and became a veteran regiment; in addition, the regiment was transferred to the V Corps, where it remained for the rest of the war. The 97th New York fought through the Overland Campaign and the Siege of Petersburg and was present at the end at Appomattox Court House. After watching the Grand Review, the regiment was mustered out near Washington on July 18, 1865, having lost during service 182 by death from wounds and 157 by death from accident, imprisonment or disease, of whom 54 died in captivity.[139]

While no official after-action report of the 97th New York's deeds at South Mountain exists, the unit history does give a dramatic account:

> *Duryee's Brigade marched along the turnpike, halting at intervals, as if it had not yet been determined where this force was most needed, till towards night it was ordered to the extreme right and marched rapidly across fields and by-roads, arriving at the base of the mountain about sunset, in position where the Pennsylvania Reserves under General Meade were engaged in an indecisive struggle with a superior Confederate force. Our arrival was most opportune, for at that critical moment the enemy had put forth all his strength in that part of the field, in a final assault; and the Union line with ammunition nearly expended, and bleeding with previous encounter, was being forced back over the ground from which they had driven the enemy.*
>
> *Our general at once ordered a charge, and with bayonets fixed and a tremendous cheer the brigade advanced to the encounter and up the mountain—with the Ninety-seventh on the right—following with cold steel the Confederate hosts.*

*Occasionally the Confederates would "about face," and fire a few
shots; but the declivity was so steep that they passed harmlessly over our
heads. About sixty of the enemy were overtaken among the rocks and
trees on the mountain slope and captured in our rapid ascent. At the
summit they made a stand, but by a well-directed fire of our line the
Confederates were soon dispersed and disappeared in the darkness down
the other slope.*[140]

One of the officers making that charge was Second Lieutenant Justus O.
Rockwell. Commissioned on March 10, 1862, in Company E of the 97th
New York Infantry, Justus Rockwell enlisted for three years and gave his
age as twenty-seven. The company descriptive book shows that Justus was
born in Trenton, New York, and was five feet, seven and three-fourth inches
tall, with a dark complexion, black eyes and black hair; he was working as a
painter prior to the war. He stated that he was living in Boonville, New York,
at the time of his enlistment.[141]

Although he was not officially mustered into service until February 1862,
Justus had enlisted with the State of New York in September 1861.[142] He
was shown as "present" from December 19, 1861, through December 31,
1861, and remained "present" with the 97th New York until his wounding
on December 13, 1862, at the Battle of Fredericksburg. The wound was
described as a "shell wound of the left foot." Prior to Fredericksburg, Justus
had been promoted to first lieutenant on October 24, 1862. He had also
commanded company E since September 1, 1862, meaning he was due extra
pay during that period. Fortunately, his wound was not serious, as Justus was
"present" in January/February 1863. He was also once again commanding
company E as of May 12, 1863.[143]

On July 1, 1863, at the Battle of Gettysburg, First Lieutenant Justus
Rockwell was captured in the railroad cut and made a prisoner of war.
Upon the retreat of the Army of Northern Virginia back to its namesake
state, Rockwell was taken along. First confined to Libby Prison in
Richmond, Virginia, after ten months he was sent to Macon, Georgia,
on May 7, 1864. Being an officer, Lieutenant Rockwell avoided being
sent to some of the most notorious prison camps, such as Camp Sumter,
better known as Andersonville. There were, however, POW camps
specifically for officers. Camp Oglethorpe, named after Georgia founder
James Oglethorpe, was one such camp. A stockaded camp on the Macon
Fairgrounds, this facility held anywhere from 600 Union officers in
1862 to 1,900 in 1864. Broken up in July 1864 due to the approach of

Left: Second Lieutenant Justus O. Rockwell, 97th New York Infantry.

Above: Back of Rockwell's image.

Union cavalry, the prisoners were distributed to other facilities.[144] It is estimated that Rockwell may have landed in Camp Asylum, another officers' prison camp, outside Columbia, South Carolina, on December 1, 1864.[145] By this point, however, the prisons' days were numbered, and it was evacuated in February 1865 due to the approach of Major General William T. Sherman.[146] Rockwell remained a prisoner until he was paroled on March 1, 1865, in North Carolina. Once paroled, Justus was sent to Camp Parole, Annapolis, Maryland, on March 9, 1865, to await discharge or to be returned to his regiment. On March 25, he was shown as a "sick" paroled POW in New York. Lieutenant Rockwell was finally discharged on June 22, 1865. In his records was a form dated July 18 noting that he had last been paid on April 30, 1863.[147] According to his pension card, Justus Rockwell filed for a pension on June 18, 1889.[148] By the 1890s, he had moved across the country and was living in Seattle, Washington, where he repeatedly ran for public office.[149] Married three times, the last time in 1930 when he was ninety-six,[150] Justus Rockwell passed away on May 25, 1932, in Seattle, Washington, and is buried at the Grand Army of the Republic Cemetery, plot 533. His widow filed for her survivor's pension on June 28, 1932.[151]

THIS IMAGE OF JUSTUS Rockwell was taken some time after 1866, following the end of the war, when Rockwell moved to Franklin, Pennsylvania. He remained in Franklin until 1878, before moving west.[152] The image has no back mark, but Rockwell signed the back, including his rank and regiment, and wrote "Franklin, Pennsylvania," so the image was probably either a gift or a calling card. The lack of a revenue tax stamp means that this was taken after August 1866, when the revenue tax on CDVs was repealed.[153]

Though seated, Justus Rockwell was provided with a table to rest his arm, as well as a steadying brace for his head. The base can be seen through the legs of the chair. Dressed in completely civilian attire, Rockwell has on a pair of light-colored pants as well as a civilian sack coat. The coat may be a touch large for him, as there appears to be a lot of material bunching around the elbows. In addition, he has some sort of vest on under the coat, as well as a cravat. Although he sports a neat goatee and mustache, as well as a nicely combed head of hair, there is something about his face. Perhaps it is his high cheekbones or the staring eyes that give an inkling of an idea that he has been through a significant ordeal.

105ᵀᴴ NEW YORK INFANTRY

Known as the Le Roy or Rochester Regiment, the 105th New York Infantry was recruited in the counties of Cattaraugus, Genesee, Monroe and Niagara. The regiment was actually a consolidation of the regiment being recruited at Rochester under Colonel Howard Carroll and the one being recruited at LeRoy under Colonel James M. Fuller. The 105th New York was mustered into United States service from November 1861 to March 1862 for three years. Leaving New York on April 4, 1862, the 105th New York was in Washington, D.C., until early May. Sent into the field, the regiment was assigned to Major General John Pope's Union Army of Virginia in late June. The 105th New York participated in the Battle of Cedar Mountain on August 9, 1862, and fought through the Second Bull Run and Maryland Campaign, losing heavily in both. The final battle of the 105th New York was in December 1862 at Fredericksburg, where it again suffered heavily.[154]

The 105th New York participated in the Mud March in early 1863, but by that point, the regiment was seriously depleted in numbers. That

March, the 105th New York was consolidated into five companies—F, G, H, I and K—and transferred to the 94th New York Infantry.[155]

There is no surviving after-action report from the 105th New York for its actions at South Mountain. However, a recent history of the battle does utilize a letter from the future commander of the regiment: "Duryee moved into the interval between Seymour and Gallagher, placing the 105th New York and the 107th Pennsylvania in his front line with fixed bayonets, and the 97th and 104th New York in support. They started up the 'almost inaccessible' mountainside as quickly as the terrain permitted with everyone 'cheering like mad men.'"[156] Captain John C. Whiteside, of the 105th New York, noted that when his regiment came under enemy fire, "we wavered and would have broken and fallen back." Captain Whiteside went on to claim he personally rallied the regiment and led it forward.[157]

The fighting at Turner's Gap fell lightly on the 105th New York, costing one enlisted man killed and two wounded, for a total of three casualties.[158] Brigadier General James Ricketts did mention several officers of the 105th New York by name in his "List of officers and men who behaved with gallantry in the engagements of September 14–17, 1862." Under the "First Brigade," he called out Lieutenant Colonel Howard Carroll, Major John W. Shedd, Captain Patrick W. Bradley and Second Lieutenant Isaac Doolittle, acting assistant adjutant to General Duryee.[159]

Among those officers listed for gallantry from the 105th New York was Captain Patrick W. Bradley of Company H. Patrick Bradley was twenty-nine years old and living in Rochester, New York, when he enlisted for three years in Company H on December 23, 1861. He was quickly recognized as a leader by his comrades and elected first lieutenant on January 10, 1862. Just over two months later, on March 25, 1862, Patrick was elected captain. His service records show him as "present" from April 30, 1862, until he was wounded on September 17, 1862, at Antietam. There are no details of the wound in his service record. The November report shows that Patrick was absent in Albany, New York. He may have been using his recovery period to recruit, as his records also state he was on duty since November 16, 1862. He remained in Albany until he returned to the regiment in February 1863. However, when the 105th New York was consolidated with the 94th New York Infantry at Belle Plain, Virginia, on March 17, 1863, Patrick was no longer needed and was mustered out of the service two days later with seventeen other officers of the former 105th New York.[160] He had last been paid on October 31, 1862.[161] Patrick filed for a pension

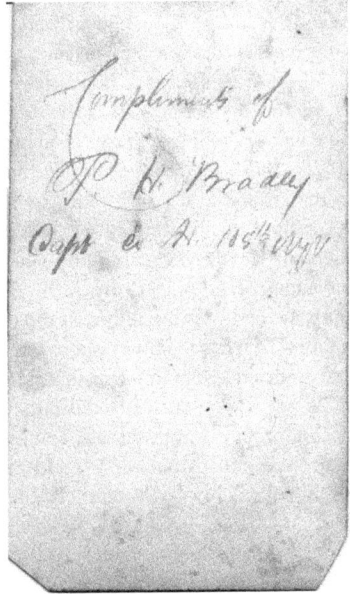

Left: Captain Patrick W. Bradley, 105th New York Infantry. *Right*: Back of Bradley's image.

on November 28, 1877, and passed away on October 10, 1880. His final resting place was not recorded.[162]

WHILE THERE IS NO back mark to identify the photographer or location of the studio, it can be speculated that Captain Patrick Bradley had this image taken in the late winter or early spring of 1862, shortly after his promotion to captain. At that time, the 105th New York was preparing to leave New York for Washington. Bradley could have had this done in New York City, as the regiment was passing through, or just as likely in Washington, as the 105th New York was posted there for almost a month after its arrival. The studio used a large column on a pedestal as both a decoration and something to brace against. It has also included a large decorative drape that spills down behind Captain Bradley's shoes, no doubt covering the feet of the brace for his head. The image itself was probably a gift, as Bradley signed "Compliments of" and listed his name, rank and regiment on the back.

For this image, the captain decided to wear almost his entire uniform—only his sword, sash and perhaps a pair of gloves are missing. Captain Bradley's shoes appear to be nicely shined, although he may have some dust or mud along the toes. He is wearing dark-blue officer's trousers with light-blue infantry piping that can just barely be seen running up the seam of his left leg. Bradley's dark-blue frock coat is very long, with the skirting coming to the knee, and has the voluminous sleeves common in an officer's frock. In addition to the nine closely spaced buttons, eight of which are visible, there are the three cuff buttons, which are visible on the left wrist and also indicative of an officer's frock. Bradley's shoulder boards, which show his rank, are easily visible, although the rank itself is difficult to make out. As an infantry captain, the board should have a light- or sky blue background with two embroidered gold bars at each end.[163]

As stated, Captain Patrick Bradley chose to wear his sword belt for this occasion, but without the usual infantry sash of crimson silk net. The belt is the standard Model 1851 field and company grade officer's belt, one and a half inches wide and made of black leather with two saber slings for carrying the officer's sword. In addition to the waist belt, Bradley has also purchased a leather shoulder strap that can be seen running from the right shoulder down to the left hip. This simple leather strap helped take the weight of the sword.[164] While there were numerous variations of the belt plate, this one is bronze, two inches wide, and appears to have the silvered laurels, which were attached separately. The scroll above the Federal eagle on the belt plate has the nation's motto, "E PLURIBUS UNUM," which should also be in silver.[165]

Atop Captain Bradley's head is his forage cap, in this case a variation of the 1858 "McDowell" cap. The short, curved, black leather visor and the leather adjusting strap with buckle are visible, as is the gold embroidered hunter's horn on the front of the forage cap. This insignia was attached to a piece of black velvet and sewn to the front of the forage cap.[166] Often the regimental number would be included in the loop of the hunter's horn, but that does not appear to be the case here. To complete his look, Patrick Bradley has also neatly trimmed his beard.

THE FIGHTING AT TURNER'S GAP ended on September 14 with Union forces in possession of the pass, ready to advance at dawn. The regiments that fought to take Turner's Gap faced very different terrain depending on where they were. Some of these men were able to advance using the National Pike and the rolling farm fields below Turner's Gap, while others had to clamber over the rocks, ledges and crumbling mountain trails to the summit.

Of the six soldiers detailed, all but one of them was wounded at some point during the war. During the fighting at Turner's Gap, Colonel Wainwright was struck; three days later at Antietam, Captain Bradley was hit. Both Captain Hendrickson and Second Lieutenant Rockwell were wounded at Fredericksburg, and Rockwell was captured seven months later at Gettysburg. His subsequent imprisonment removed him from the war. Colonel Fairchild was wounded and briefly captured at Gettysburg as well but was quickly released. Only Major Madill avoided bleeding for the Union cause, and as a surgeon, he was continually trying to aid and comfort those who were wounded. While several of these men and their regiments were only lightly engaged at South Mountain, these I Corps regiments were destined to be in the thick of the fighting in many battles to come.

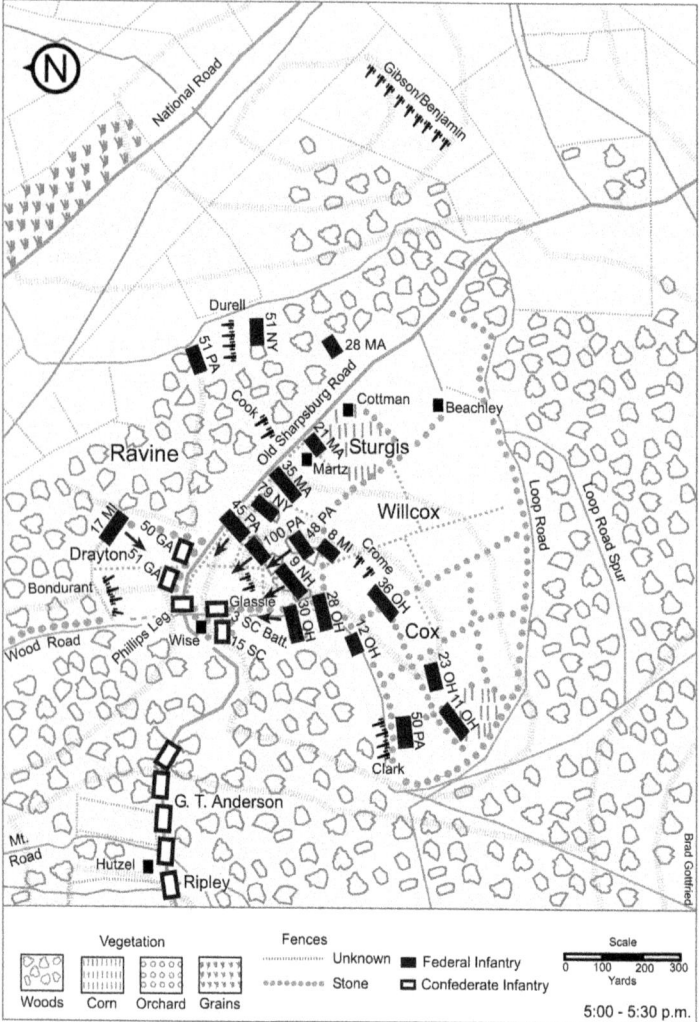

South Mountain—Fox's Gap, 5:00 p.m.–5:30 p.m. *Map provided by Dr. Bradley Gottfried.*

Chapter 3

FOX'S GAP

The Battle of South Mountain actually began at Fox's Gap sometime before 9:00 a.m. on September 14, 1862. By 6:00 a.m. that morning, the Union IX Corps, commanded by Major General Jesse Reno, was advancing from its bivouac west of Middletown, Maryland, in the wake of Federal cavalry moving along the National Road. The lead division of the IX Corps as it approached South Mountain was the Kanawha Division of Ohio regiments, commanded by Brigadier General Jacob Cox. General Cox in his report stated, "At 6 o'clock in the morning of September 14 the division marched from Middletown under an order received by me from Major General Reno directing me to support with my division the advance of General Pleasanton, who, with his brigade of cavalry and artillery, was moving up the Hagerstown turnpike toward the positions of the enemy in the pass of South Mountain."[167]

As the cavalry skirmished with Confederate pickets near Turner's Gap, it became clear that the gap was held in force and that an alternative approach was needed. As the Federal troops approached the small crossroads community of Bolivar, the lead brigade, commanded by Colonel Eliakim Scammon, turned left off the National Pike to reach the Old Sharpsburg Road, which cut through Fox's Gap. The intention was to outflank the Confederate position at Turner's Gap, about one mile to the north of Fox's Gap. Under the cover of Union artillery deployed on rising ground southeast of Turner's Gap, the IX Corps struggled up the road leading to the gap.

The fighting at Fox's Gap began with the units of Scammon's Brigade trying to move farther south to flank the Confederate defenders at Fox's Gap. Led by the 23rd Ohio Infantry, these Federals utilized the Loop Road and its spur to work their way up South Mountain. The fighting that erupted that morning was costly to both sides but succeeded in pushing Confederate troops away from the Ridge Road at the top of South Mountain and back from Fox's Gap itself. By noon, both sides were spent, and the Wise Farm in Fox's Gap became something of a no-man's-land. For the next two hours, both Union and Confederate reinforcements were shifted to Fox's Gap, and the fighting resumed around 2:00 p.m. By 5:00 p.m., both sides had arrived in force, and a pitched engagement around Wise Farm ensued. Looking at the map from west to east, the units to be examined were as follows. On the left of Major General Jacob Cox's Division was the 23rd Ohio Infantry from Colonel Eliakim Scammon's Brigade. Farther east, leading the advance, was the 30th Ohio Infantry, also from Colonel Scammon's Brigade. To its immediate right was the 46th New York Infantry from Colonel Thomas Welsh's Brigade of Brigadier General Orlando Willcox's Division. From the same brigade and moving up the Old Sharpsburg Road was the 45th Pennsylvania Infantry. Behind the 45th Pennsylvania, coming up the Old Sharpsburg Road in support, was the 21st Massachusetts Infantry from Brigadier General Edward Ferrero's Brigade of Brigadier General Samuel D. Sturgis's Division. On the extreme east of the attack was the brand-new 17th Michigan Infantry, assigned to Colonel Benjamin Christ's Brigade.

23RD OHIO INFANTRY

The 23rd Ohio Infantry was organized at Camp Chase in Columbus, Ohio, on June 1, 1861. The 23rd Ohio is best remembered for having two future presidents in its ranks: Rutherford B. Hayes and William McKinley. The regiment was mustered into service on June 11, 1861, and left the state that July for western Virginia. On September 10, 1861, the 23rd Ohio took part in its first major action at Canifex Ferry in western Virginia. After a brief pursuit, the 23rd Ohio went into winter quarters at Camp Ewing on the New River, where it suffered significantly from sickness. With the opening of the spring campaign in 1862, the 23rd Ohio was attacked in its camp by a Confederate brigade and driven back to New River before being reinforced. It returned to the site of the attack at Flat Top Mountain and remained there until ordered east on July 13, arriving in Washington on August 24, 1862. With the reorganization of Federal forces under Major General George McClellan during the first days of September, the 23rd Ohio became part of the Union IX Corps and took part in the battles of South Mountain and Antietam.[168]

Following the Maryland Campaign, the division of Brigadier General Jacob Cox, including the 23rd Ohio, was ordered back to the Kanawha Valley in October 1862. In March 1863, the regiment was ordered to Charleston, (West) Virginia. The 23rd Ohio remained in the area of Charleston until May 1864, when it took part in the Army of West Virginia's campaign against the Virginia and Tennessee Railroad that resulted in the Battle of Cloyd's Mountain. After this, the Army of West Virginia began the long march that culminated in Major General David Hunter's failed Lynchburg Campaign. Retreating from Lynchburg, the 23rd Ohio fought at the Second Battle of Kernstown in July 1864; again at Berryville, Virginia, that August; and then participated in the successful Shenandoah Valley Campaign of Major General Philip Sheridan that fall, which concluded with the Battle of Cedar Creek on October 19, 1864. At the end of the campaign, the 23rd Ohio was sent back to West Virginia for the winter and mustered out on July 26, 1865.[169]

Leading the attack on Fox's Gap, the 23rd Ohio was on left of the Union line during the fighting on September 14, 1862. The regiment entered the Battle of South Mountain with an unknown number of men. Colonel Eliakim P. Scammon, in his report of the battle, wrote, "I ordered the Twenty-third Regiment, under Lieutenant-Colonel Hayes, to move through the woods on the left of the road, crossing the mountain so as to attack the enemy on the right and rear of the right flank. The regiment moved up promptly and effectively. Early in the encounter, Lieutenant-Colonel Hayes, commanding the regiment, who had gallantly and skillfully brought his men into action and charged the enemy in his front, was severely wounded and carried to the rear. He remained on the field a considerable time after receiving his wound, and left it only when compelled to retire."[170]

The fighting at Fox's Gap on South Mountain was a hard day for the 23rd Ohio Infantry. Following the battle, the regiment reported losses of 32 enlisted men killed, 8 officers and 87 enlisted wounded and 3 missing, for a total of 130.[171]

One of those caught up in the intense fighting for Fox's Gap was First Sergeant Amos F. Gillis. Amos, along with his brothers Allen and James, joined Company B of the 23rd Ohio Infantry on June 2, 1861. He gave his age as twenty-three and signed up for three years of service.[172] Of Amos, born in Kinsman, Ohio, the Company B descriptive book stated that he was five feet, eleven inches tall; had a light complexion, blue eyes and dark hair; and was a bookkeeper before the war. For most of his first month of service, Amos was "present sick in quarters." After this, Amos was listed as "present" until November/December 1862. During this period, Amos Gillis was promoted to corporal on August 25, 1861; he was promoted again to fourth sergeant on October 19, 1861, and on March 1, 1862, to first sergeant. During the November/December 1862 period, Amos was detached from his regiment and sent to Ohio on recruiting duty. With the turn of the year, Amos was promoted again, this time to second lieutenant, on January 24, 1863. Now an officer, he commanded Company B from March 16 to August 1, 1863. At the end of 1863, Lieutenant Gillis was detached again on December 30, for another round of recruiting duty. This did not last long, however, as Gillis was present again in January/February 1864. In June 1864, Amos was on special duty commanding the company as of June 9, 1864. While in command of the company, Gillis was promoted to first lieutenant on June 14, 1864. Finally, on July 7, 1864, Amos received his promotion to captain and was transferred to Company H. That same month, Amos was briefly captured near Winchester, Virginia, following the Second Battle of Kernstown:[173]

> *Here A.F. Gillis was taken prisoner, but escaped, getting back within our lines after undergoing many hardships, wandering about he knew not where, traveling nights and concealing himself during the day-time, ten days, until so nearly starved that he thought it better to give himself up as a prisoner again rather than die of starvation. On coming forth from his place of concealment, and giving himself up as he supposed to a rebel, great was his surprise at finding him a Union man.*[174]

Sadly, Amos Gillis's return to the 23rd Ohio was brief, as he was killed in action on September 3, 1864, at Berryville, Virginia. After he was struck in the heart by a Confederate bullet, Captain Amos Gillis's last words were, "Boys, carry me back." Fortunately for his family, Amos's brother James was allowed to escort his remains back to Ohio. Today, Amos Gillis rests at Kinsman Cemetery, Kinsman, Ohio.[175] His name is also listed on the 23rd Ohio Infantry monument in Woodland Cemetery in Cleveland, Ohio.[176]

Left: First Sergeant Amos F. Gillis, 23rd Ohio Infantry. *Right*: Back of Gillis's image.

THE NAME A.A. UDALL does not appear in the company records of the 23rd Ohio. However, Addison A. Udell of Company B, 23rd Ohio Infantry, does.[177] A photographer both before and after the war,[178] it is quite possible that during the winter of 1863, then Corporal Udell (or Udall) set up shop in Charleston, Virginia, to make some money on the side as a photographer for his regiment. One of his apparent customers was Amos Gillis, who had this bust image taken after his promotion to the rank of second lieutenant. The 23rd Ohio was ordered to Charleston, Virginia, in March 1863 and remained there until July. As Amos has both his coat and vest open, probably for ventilation, it is possible that this was taken in the spring or early summer of 1863, prior to the 23rd Ohio being ordered back into the field. The image itself was signed by Gillis and may have been a calling card or gift, as it includes his rank and regiment.

In this photo, Second Lieutenant Amos Gillis is wearing an officer's dark-blue frock coat. The frock has a standing collar as well as nine large, evenly spaced Federal eagle buttons, seven of which are visible.[179] His shoulder boards, the indicators of his rank, are also visible. In this case, the boards are empty of any decoration, thus indicating a second lieutenant, with only a light-blue interior signifying infantry.[180] The vest itself appears to be a dark-blue officer's vest. These usually had nine buttons,[181] and seven of the small eagle buttons can be seen in this image. Amos Gillis is also wearing a black cravat, the only color allowed by regulation, which can be seen just above his topmost coat button,[182] as well as a freshly starched shirt or a new paper collar. As the CDV has faded, it is difficult to make out some details, but Second Lieutenant Gillis may have a subtle mustache to go with his mutton chops and disheveled head of hair.

30TH OHIO INFANTRY

The 30th Ohio Infantry was organized in Columbus, Ohio, at Camp Chase on August 28, 1861, to serve for three years. Immediately armed and equipped, the regiment was ordered to the field on August 30. The 30th Ohio had its first dress parade on Christmas Day 1861 at Fayetteville, (West) Virginia, where the regiment went into winter quarters. Fortifications were built and outposts manned during that period. On April 17, 1862, the 30th Ohio broke camp and headed for Raleigh, (West) Virginia. The regiment helped determine the size and position of Confederate forces in western Virginia before being brigaded with other Ohio regiments on May 17. Now part of the 1st Brigade of Brigadier General Jacob Cox's Kanawha Division, the 30th Ohio was sent to Great Flat Top Mountain. On August 16, 1862, orders were received to move east to join the Federal troops under Major General John Pope. Arriving at Warrenton Junction, Virginia, on August 23, the 30th Ohio was divided, with the right wing of the regiment acting as Pope's headquarters guard, while the left wing was reassigned to the brigade of Brigadier General John C. Robinson, under whom they fought at Second Bull Run. The regiment was returned to the 1st Brigade of the Kanawha Division in time for the Maryland Campaign and fought hard at South Mountain and Antietam, losing significantly at both. Following the Maryland Campaign, the Kanawha Division, the 30th Ohio with it, was ordered back to western Virginia.[183]

Though initially ordered into winter quarters, the 30th Ohio was not there long. The regiment was ordered west, reaching Louisville, Kentucky, on January 3, 1863. Moving down the Ohio and Mississippi Rivers, the

30th Ohio reached Helena, Arkansas, and was assigned to the XV Corps. The 30th Ohio Infantry went on to participate in the Siege of Vicksburg. That fall, the regiment participated in the relief of Chattanooga and the Battle of Missionary Ridge on November 25, 1863. The spring of 1864 saw the opening of the Atlanta Campaign, in which the 30th Ohio participated until the fall of Atlanta on September 2, 1864. The 30th Ohio continued on the March to the Sea and was with the forces that took Fort McAllister on December 13, 1864, forcing the evacuation of Savannah. After this, the regiment served in the Carolinas Campaign. Following the surrender of Confederate General Joseph Johnston, the 30th Ohio was retained on guard duty until August 13, 1865, when it was sent home and mustered out.[184]

During the fighting at Fox's Gap, the 30th Ohio advanced up South Mountain and became heavily engaged, as reported by Colonel Eliakim P. Scammon in his write-up of the battle:

> *On arriving at the foot of the slope in front of the enemy, I sent the Thirtieth Regiment, commanded by Colonel Hugh Ewing, to attack the left of that position of the enemy which was immediately opposed to us, with orders, if practicable, to seize a battery in that part of the enemy's lines. In executing this order, it was ascertained that the battery was beyond reach, and that its infantry support far outnumbered the force opposed to it; but the Thirtieth Regiment attacked vigorously and drove the enemy from their immediate front. They were assailed by a shower of grape from the battery, whose real position and strength were not previously known, but they seized and held the crest of the mountain until they nobly bore their part in the charge by our whole line. In all this I am happy to say there was no faltering. It was the thorough work of good soldiers.*[185]

The fighting at Fox's Gap cost the 30th Ohio seventeen enlisted killed, fifty-three enlisted wounded and no missing, for a total of seventy casualties.[186]

Advancing into Fox's Gap on September 14, 1862, was Corporal Mathias T. Hamilton of Company I. Hamilton enlisted in the 30th Ohio Infantry as a private on September 2, 1861, for three years. At the time, he stated he was twenty-six years old and working as a farmer. Mathias was noted in the company descriptive book as being five feet, seven inches tall with blue eyes, auburn hair and a fair complexion. As was common with the records of this period, his status was "not stated" until February 28, 1862. On February 6, Mathias was promoted to corporal, and he received a twenty-day furlough on February 26. Corporal Hamilton was "present" from March/April 1862 to May/June 1863, when he was reported as "absent" on guard duty at Young's Point, Louisiana, as of May 13, 1863. Mathias returned to the 30th Ohio during the July/August period and was "present" for the rest of his service. When he reenlisted in January 1864, he received $19.08 for a clothing allowance, a $100 bounty and a veteran's furlough. Right at the end of the war on April 13, 1865, Hamilton was promoted to sergeant and then again on May 20 to quartermaster sergeant. Mathias mustered out of the service on August 13, 1865, at Little Rock, Arkansas; he had last been paid on April 30. Although he had drawn $51.52 against his clothing allowance over the course of his service, Mathias was still due $210 of his bounty when he mustered out.[187] Mathias filed for a pension on April 26, 1882.[188] It was finally awarded five years later in early August 1887, when Mathias was living in Indiana.[189] Mathias T. Hamilton passed away on September 27, 1908, and is buried at Goodwill Cemetery, Loogootee, Indiana.[190]

TAKEN AT THE PHOTOGRAPHIC gallery of Reeve & Watts in Columbus, Ohio, this image of Mathias T. Hamilton was likely done shortly after his enlistment in August 1861. This is due to his lack of uniform, as well as no indication of rank in his signature. As Hamilton signed the front of this CDV with his name, company and regiment, it is likely that this was meant as a calling card or perhaps as a gift for someone to remember him by as he entered the service. A previous collector included on the back of the image his regiment, along with his full name and the dates of his various promotions. Interestingly, they also included his muster-in date of September 2, 1861, when his enlistment was recognized by the United States government.[191]

Mathias T. Hamilton is wearing his civilian attire in this image. A light coat over a dark-blue or black vest, unbuttoned except for the topmost. He has a high, stiff collar, possibly a paper collar, and may have on a cravat, although his beard covers where the knot would be. With a set jaw, neatly trimmed beard, combed and oiled hair and a determined gaze, Mathias Hamilton looks ready for his service.

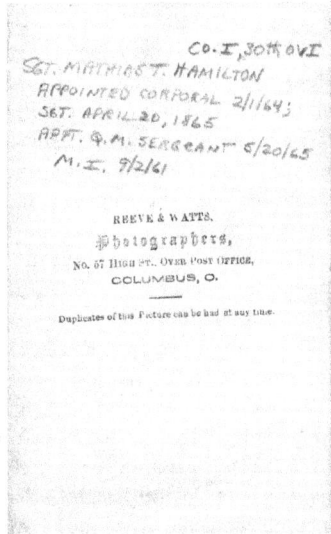

Left: Private Mathias T. Hamilton, 30ᵗʰ Ohio Infantry. *Right*: Back of Hamilton's image.

46ᵀᴴ NEW YORK INFANTRY

Known as the Fremont Rifle Regiment, the 46ᵗʰ New York Infantry was composed of German Americans and named after the Republican hero Major General John C. Frémont. Though recruiting began in New York City, the regiment had men of German ancestry from Brooklyn and Albany, New York, as well as Baltimore, Maryland, and Washington.[192] The 46ᵗʰ New York mustered into the service of the United States from July 29 to September 16, 1861, for a three-year term. On September 16, 1861, the regiment, now eight hundred strong, left for Washington. Assigned to the 1ˢᵗ Brigade of Brigadier General Thomas W. Sherman's Division and quartered at Annapolis, the 46ᵗʰ New York was ordered to the Department of the South in November and wintered on Tybee Island, Georgia. During this time, the regiment took part in the Siege of Fort Pulaski. Ordered to James Island, South Carolina, in June, the 46ᵗʰ New York took part in the Battle of Secessionville in July 1862. It was then ordered to return to Newport News, Virginia, where the regiment was assigned to the 2nd Brigade, 1st Division, IX Corps, with which it took part in the Battles of Sulphur Springs, Second Bull Run, Chantilly, South Mountain and Antietam. In reserve at Fredericksburg, the 46th New York wintered at Falmouth, Virginia. The IX Corps was ordered west in 1863 and joined the operations against Vicksburg, Mississippi, in June. After the capitulation of Vicksburg, the IX Corps was ordered to Knoxville, Tennessee, and was engaged at Blue Spring and Campbell's Station. The 46th New York endured the Confederate Siege of Knoxville from September to December 1863, and a majority of the regiment reenlisted that winter, making it a veteran regiment. Upon the veterans' return from furlough in the spring of 1864, the 46th New York was transferred briefly to the V Corps before being returned to the IX Corps. No longer out west, the IX Corps served with the Army of the Potomac through the Overland Campaign and the Siege of Petersburg that followed. With the fall of Petersburg, the 46th New York was ordered to Washington, where it was mustered out on July 28, 1865.[193]

Lieutenant Colonel Joseph Gerhardt, who commanded the 46th New York at South Mountain, wrote the following in his official report:

> *As soon as the enemy commenced to assail us with musketry fire, the regiment went up to a stone fence, where it remained until further orders. Receiving orders, the regiment went over the fence under a very heavy fire of musketry and advanced in line of battle to the woods, where the Twenty-eighth Ohio Regiment were lying behind a rail fence. I ordered the regiment to assist our brothers in the fight, and with hurrah and double-quick they came to the relief of the Thirtieth Ohio, leaving the Twenty-eighth Ohio Volunteers behind us, who had been relieved by the Thirtieth Ohio Regiment. Both officers and men behaved gallantly in this engagement, taking proper advantages of coverings at hand, to which is attributable the small loss we sustained.[194]*

Compared with the casualties in other Union regiments, the 46th New York's losses at Fox's Gap were indeed light. The regiment reported two enlisted killed, one officer and six enlisted wounded and no missing, for a total of nine.[195]

One of the many German immigrants in the 46th New York that day was Captain Theodore Hohle. Born in 1828 in Germany, Theodore Hohle immigrated to the United States on December 16, 1853.[196] At the outbreak of the war, Hohle was thirty-three years old and mustered into Company A of the 46th New York Infantry on July 29, 1861. He enlisted for three years of service and mustered in as a second lieutenant. On September 2, Hohle was promoted to first lieutenant and promoted again on September 23, 1861, to captain of Company H. Starting in September, Theodore was listed as "present" in his service records and remained so until after the Battle of Antietam. Captain Hohle was detached on September 20, 1862, for recruiting duty in New York City, replacing Captain Anton Hinckel, who had broken his leg. Recalled from New York on January 5, 1863, Captain Hohle was promoted again, this time to major. On July 27, 1863, Major Hohle was discharged for ill health, described as typhoid fever and diarrhea. Theodore went to a hospital in Cincinnati, the Marine General Hospital, where he died on September 5, 1863.[197] Major Theodore Hohle is buried at Spring Grove Cemetery in Cincinnati, Ohio, Grave 21B-202.[198]

TAKEN IN NEW YORK City, this image of Theodore Hohle was done in the gallery of photographer Adolph Hohle. It is very likely that these two men were related, as they immigrated to the United States together in 1853 aboard the ship *Union*.[199] No specific familial connection has been discovered, however. Posted to New York City for recruiting duty on September 20, 1862, it appears that then Captain Theodore Hohle was made aware of his impending promotion to major prior to his return to the regiment. This was probably done to allow Hohle the opportunity to update his uniform prior to his return. Theodore Hohle took advantage of this and had his image taken in his major's uniform

Setting up this image, photographer Hohle provided a short table with decorative covering for use as a stand for Theodore Hohle's hat. He also placed a brace behind the major to keep his head steady during the exposure—the feet and upright of the brace can be clearly seen behind Hohle's right leg. This standing image of Theodore Hohle shows off his nearly complete uniform. On his feet are likely ankle boots, although it is difficult to tell due to the regulation to have trousers fall over the top of any footwear.[200] With the smooth side of the leather facing out, they have been shined nicely for the image. His trousers are dark blue, with the eighth-of-an-inch light-blue piping just barely visible running up the seam of Hohle's left leg. This signifies an infantry officer, but this uniform requirement was superseded by General Orders No. 108, allowing infantry officers to wear the sky blue trousers similar to the enlisted, with dark-blue piping, if they so wished after December 1861.[201]

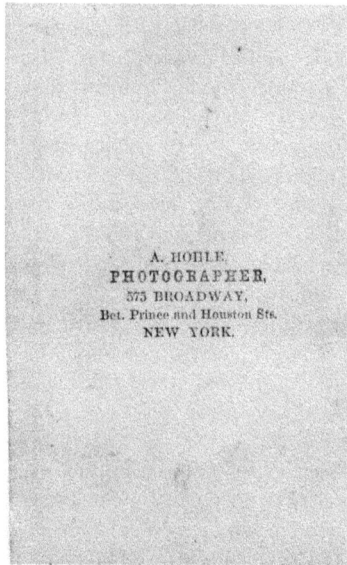

Left: Captain Theodore Hohle, 46th New York Infantry. *Right*: Back of Hohle's image.

The double-breasted frock coat worn by Theodore Hohle bears several indicators of him being a high-ranking officer. The coat itself is dark blue and has the traditional skirting of a frock coat. It is interesting to note the length of the skirting here, as officers' frocks tended to be longer; however, it still has the voluminous sleeves and three cuff buttons on each wrist—all indications of an officer.[202] Across his chest is a double row on seven buttons, evenly spaced; six of the buttons are visible in this image, with the seventh of each row being under his waist belt. This configuration of buttons is used on the senior officers of a regiment: the colonel, lieutenant colonel and major.[203] In the case of Theodore Hohle's buttons, he actually has two different types. The first four buttons in his right row all have a distinct ring design and are very likely New York State seal buttons. The last two buttons in that same row and several in the left row appear to be the large Federal eagle buttons.[204] The uppermost buttons in the left row appear to be larger as well, but it is difficult to tell if they are the state seal buttons or not. Finally, on each of Hohle's shoulders are his shoulder boards. In this case, Major Hohle has likely paid extra for the thick (about 0.375 inches) gold embroidered border of his shoulder boards.[205] Though washed out in this image, these boards had a light-blue interior with a gold oak leaf at each end, the symbol for a major.[206]

Theodore Hohle is also wearing his sword belt and saber for this image; for an infantry officer, the sword was another symbol of rank. In this case, he is likely using the same belt and sword he had as a lieutenant and captain. Neither piece is particularly flamboyant and the sword belt is mostly covered, but what can be seen is plain black leather, probably about 1.5 inches wide, with two 1-inch saber slings, which are attached to his scabbard in this image. His belt plate appears to be a variation on the standard 2-inch-wide rectangular plate with raised rim. The Arms of the United States, an eagle with wings splayed, is apparent on the plate, but there is no indication of the silvered wreath or scroll.[207] As for the sword itself, it is a very utilitarian—a nearly straight-bladed version of a foot officer's saber. This particular saber is non-regulation, which can be seen by its open guard design. The iron scabbard is lacking the decorative throat of an 1850 field officer's saber but still has the two carrying rings and a drag at the end.[208] Draped around the guard is a non-regulation sword knot. As opposed to a gold lace strap with gold bullion tassel, this sword knot appears to be a simple leather strap with a nondescript tassel.[209]

Sitting on the table next to Theodore Hohle is his hat. Like his belt and sword, this porkpie hat may be a holdover from an earlier rank. Although a regulation calls for a gold embroidered bugle with the regimental numbers in the loop, Major Hohle has either a gold or silver laurel wreath with the number "46" displayed prominently between the wings of the laurel. The crown of his low hat is encircled with a cord, in this case the black silk and gold cord with acorn tassels used by officers.[210]

To finish off his image, Theodore Hohle is wearing a new paper collar, which can be seen above the high collar of his frock. In addition, and according to the regulations of the army, Hohle has neatly combed his hair, sweeping it back from his forehead, as well as trimmed his mustache and goatee.[211] He presents a fantastic appearance for his CDV and wears a look of confidence.

45TH PENNSYLVANIA INFANTRY

The 45th Pennsylvania Infantry was recruited in the counties of Center, Lancaster, Mifflin, Tioga and Wayne. The regiment was recruited from July 28 to October 18, 1861, and mustered into United States service for three years on October 21, 1861, at Camp Curtin, Harrisburg, Pennsylvania. Shipped off to Washington, the 45th Pennsylvania arrived two days later and camped on the Bladensburg Road. On November 19, the regiment embarked for Fortress Monroe, Virginia, where it remained at Camp Hamilton until December 6. At that time, the 45th Pennsylvania, along with comrades in the 76th Pennsylvania, sailed for Port Royal, South Carolina. This occupation continued into the new year. The 45th Pennsylvania continued to occupy the coastal islands, launching various raids and patrols prior to taking part in the overland maneuvers against Charleston, South Carolina, in June 1862 and acting as the rearguard during the Battle of Secessionville on June 16, 1862. On July 18, the 45th Pennsylvania was moved to Hilton Head, South Carolina, in preparation for its return to Fortress Monroe, which occurred on July 21, 1862.[212]

In early August 1862, the 45th Pennsylvania was with the 1st Brigade, 1st Division, IX Corps, in Northern Virginia. On September 6, the regiment joined the Army of the Potomac on the Maryland Campaign. The regiment fought at the Battle of South Mountain and were lightly engaged at Antietam. They were fortunate to be in reserve at Fredericksburg and camped at Falmouth, Virginia, until February 1863, when they were sent to Newport News. Ordered west, the 45th Pennsylvania arrived in Jamestown, Kentucky, on June 1, 1863. The IX Corps participated in the Siege of Vicksburg before proceeding to East Tennessee. The 45th Pennsylvania was engaged at Blue Springs, Tennessee, prior to defending Knoxville during the Confederate siege from September to December 1863. During the winter of 1864, the 45th Pennsylvania reenlisted as a veteran regiment. In May 1864, the 45th Pennsylvania was back in the East, coordinating with the Army of the Potomac during the Overland Campaign and the Siege of Petersburg that followed. That summer, the 45th Pennsylvania was at Poplar Spring Church, where a portion of the regiment was surrounded and, after a desperate attempt to fight their way clear, captured. Filled with recruits, the regiment participated in the action at Hatcher's Run in October 1864 and in the final assault on Petersburg, Virginia, on April 2, 1865. Taking part in the pursuit of Lee's Army of Northern Virginia to Appomattox and later the Grand

Review in Washington, the 45[213] Pennsylvania mustered out in Alexandria, Virginia, on July 17, 1865.[213]

In his official report of the fighting at Fox's Gap during the Battle of South Mountain, the 45th Pennsylvania's Colonel Thomas Welsh wrote the following:

> *Arriving in the crest, it encountered the enemy, also advancing—Notwithstanding the terrific fire from infantry and artillery, together with a raking fire from a battery near the turnpike, our troops continued to advance, utterly regardless of the slaughter in their ranks, until, having destroyed the advanced troops of the enemy, he was compelled to give way and retreat with his artillery and infantry in great confusion down the hill.—The ammunition of the Forty-fifth Pennsylvania Volunteers having become expended, they used the bayonet with success, and having become considerably exhausted by their extraordinary exertions, I withdrew my command as fast as relieved by troops of General Sturgis' command.*[214]

At South Mountain, the 45th Pennsylvania reported losses of 2 officers and 25 enlisted killed, 5 officers and 102 enlisted wounded and no missing, for a total of 134.[215]

Having recruited twenty men to join Company F of the 45th Pennsylvania Infantry, George P. Scudder of Equinunk, Pennsylvania, was commissioned second lieutenant of the company on October 16, 1861.[216] At the time, George was twenty-one years old and five feet, eight inches tall, with a dark complexion, black eyes and black hair. He stated that he was born in Prattsville, New York, and worked as a farmer before the war. Having joined for three years at Harrisburg, Pennsylvania, his service records show him "present" until September/October 1863. During his early months of service, he was assigned as acting as aide-de-camp on Brigadier General Oliver O. Howard's staff November 1–19, 1861. Due to the resignation of the first lieutenant of Company F, George Scudder was promoted to first lieutenant on April 21, 1862, the rank he held at the Battle of South Mountain later that fall. Rank did have its privileges, and in July/ August 1863, George was absent for ten days on leave. On October 26, 1863, he was detached on recruiting duty at Knoxville, Tennessee, by order of Major General Ambrose Burnside. Upon his return, he was next detailed as assistant provost marshal for 1st Brigade, 1st Division, IX Corps, on November 14, 1863. George was returned to the 45th Pennsylvania on January 16, 1864. Lieutenant Scudder was reassigned to recruiting duty from March 10 through April 30, 1864, by order of General Burnside. It is noted, however, that he had returned to the regiment on May 26, 1864. The final entry in his service records states that George Scudder had been placed in command of Company H, as it lacked any officers, and that he was killed in action on June 3, 1864, at the Battle of Cold Harbor, Virginia, just eight days after his return to the regiment.[217]

While details are limited, it appears that during the battle at Cold Harbor, Companies G and H were in a ravine at a right angle to the Confederate line. The fire directed down the ravine was terrible, and all the noncommissioned officers of Company H save one were cut down. At this point, Lieutenant Scudder, temporarily in command of the company, was mortally wounded and died on the field. Interestingly, the history of the 45th Pennsylvania notes that the younger brother of George Scudder, Macaiah Scudder, who was working for a sutler, visited the 45th Pennsylvania while in the siege lines of Petersburg in July 1864. The young man was allowed "to fire a shot at the Johnnies, which he did," after which "[w]e returned to camp, Scudder having the satisfaction of firing a shot at the enemy who had caused the death of his brother."[218] First Lieutenant George P. Scudder is buried at Richmond National Cemetery, Section 7A, Plot 1597.[219]

THIS PHOTOGRAPH OF GEORGE P. Scudder was taken by a C.D. Fredricks and Company photographer, apparently in New York City. The famous photography studio used the entire back of the image for advertising. This large but still relatively simple design was popular from about 1863 to 1869.[220] Although it is difficult to make out, George Scudder appears to be a second lieutenant in this image. He mustered into service as a second lieutenant in the fall of 1861 and was promoted to first lieutenant in April 1862. Although his records do not mention a trip to New York during this period, perhaps he went prior to the 45th Pennsylvania Infantry shipping out to Washington, or perhaps he was on an errand for an officer prior to the 45th Pennsylvania heading to the South Carolina coast. Although Scudder was sent on recruiting details later in the war and was on furlough in the winter of 1864, giving him opportunity to have this image taken, it seems unlikely that he would have not worn his proper rank for his CDV. It is far more likely that this is an early war image and that the well-known C.D. Fredricks photography studio was an early adopter to advertising on the backs of its images.

Left: First Lieutenant George P. Scudder, 45th Pennsylvania Infantry. *Right*: Back of Scudder's image.

A three-quarter-length standing view, Lieutenant George Scudder steadies himself using a small table provided to display his forage cap. Dominating the image is Scudder's dark-blue officer's frock coat. The coat has the large sleeves often seen on officers' frocks, a short standing collar and nine large Federal eagle buttons running down the front. Six of these buttons are visible, and the buttonholes for the three buttons behind his hand can also be seen. Scudder has unbuttoned the three to give himself access to the frock coat's internal breast pocket, for a more relaxed look. The three small eagle cuff buttons can also be seen on his right wrist. As implied earlier, Scudder's shoulder boards have been washed out by the exposure, but on close examination, there does not appear to be anything within the borders of the shoulder boards. The light-blue interior of the boards and lack of insignia designates George Scudder as a second lieutenant of infantry.[221]

Sitting beside his left hand is Lieutenant Scudder's forage cap, on the face of which is a gold embroidered hunter's horn on a black velvet patch. It is difficult to tell, but the "45" for the 45th Pennsylvania can just be seen within the loop of the horn.[222] The cap itself appears to be a standard Model 1858 made of dark-blue wool, with a dark-blue welt around the crown, a leather visor and adjustable leather strap.[223] George Scudder also took his time to trim his full beard and mustache and comb his hair for this image.

21ST MASSACHUSETTS INFANTRY

The 21st Massachusetts Infantry was made up of companies raised in the central and western part of Massachusetts in the summer of 1861. The regiment was organized at Camp Lincoln, named for former Massachusetts governor Levi Lincoln, in Worcester, Massachusetts. The majority of the 21st Massachusetts was mustered into the service of the United States on August 16, for three years of service, while the officers were commissioned through August 21. The 21st Massachusetts arrived in Baltimore, Maryland, on August 25 and remained there for several days before being sent to Annapolis, Maryland, arriving on August 30, 1861. The regiment remained in and about the area until January 9, 1862, when it departed to join the Burnside Expedition to North Carolina aboard the steamer *Northerner*.[224]

The 21st Massachusetts was assigned to the 2nd Brigade of the Coast Division and fought at Roanoke Island on February 8, New Bern on March 14 and Camden on April 19, 1862. It returned north on August 5, when the regiment embarked for Newport News, Virginia. The regiment was reassigned to the newly formed IX Corps and took part in Major General John Pope's campaign in Northern Virginia. That fall, the 21st Massachusetts fought at Second Bull Run, Chantilly, South Mountain, Antietam and Fredericksburg before going into winter quarters at Falmouth, Virginia. On February 9, 1863, the IX Corps was ordered west to Kentucky. Later that year, the regiment took part in the defense of Knoxville, Tennessee, which was under Confederate siege. With the siege broken in December, the majority of the regiment reenlisted. Following their veterans' furlough, the 21st Massachusetts was reorganized at Annapolis, Maryland, on March 20, 1864. With the IX Corps, the regiment took part in the Overland Campaign and the Siege of Petersburg. Due to casualties and expiration of enlistments, the regiment was reduced to a battalion of three companies on August 18, 1864. Following the Battle of Poplar Spring Church, the battalion was transferred to the 56th Massachusetts Infantry and mustered out with that regiment on July 12, 1865.[225]

Brigadier General Edward Ferrero, who commanded the brigade in which the 21st Massachusetts fought at Fox's Gap, reported the following:

> *At about 3.30 o'clock I advanced, by your orders, to the top of the heights in advance of our other forces, and was unexpectedly fired upon from the woods by a large force of the enemy. The sudden fire produced the utmost confusion in one of my new regiments. It quickly recovered, however, reforming under a severe fire. My command then advanced, and after a long and hard fight, lasting until 9 p.m., drove the enemy from their position and occupied the field. We retained possession of the battle-field during the night, having our whole force on guard, momentarily expecting a renewal of the attack. The enemy posted their pickets within a few yards of our lines, and during the night quietly withdrew their main body. We captured above 100 prisoners.*
>
> *In this battle all the troops of my command behaved with the greatest bravery. I have to mention as worthy of particular praise the conduct of the Fifty-first New York Volunteers, commanded by Lieutenant Colonel R.B. Potter; the Fifty-first Pennsylvania Volunteers, commanded by Colonel J.F. Hartranft, and the Twenty-first Massachusetts Volunteers, commanded by Colonel W.S. Clark. Colonel E.A. Wild, of the Thirty-fifth Massachusetts Volunteers, was wounded severely in the arm while forming his regiment under the enemy's fire. I append a list of the killed and wounded in this engagement, amounting to 10 killed, 83 wounded, 23 missing; total, 116.[226]*

One of the officers in the 21st Massachusetts struggling up South Mountain at Fox's Gap was Theodore Samuel Foster. Born in Brattleboro, Vermont, Theodore Foster was a thirty-five-year-old blacksmith living in Fitchburg, Massachusetts, when the war broke out. Commissioned on July 19, 1861, Theodore was mustered into Company D as its captain on August 21, 1861. His service records show he was "present" until the roll of February 28, 1862, when he was shown as being in the General Hospital. Theodore was Wounded in Action on February 8, 1862, at Roanoke Island. The wound was described as "leg broken, slight."[227] The regimental history of the 21st Massachusetts goes into more detail, however, describing the wound as "struck in the leg by a bullet which broke and badly splintered the bone; and, although by unflinching determination and endurance he saved his leg from amputation, it has cost him long years of suffering." For

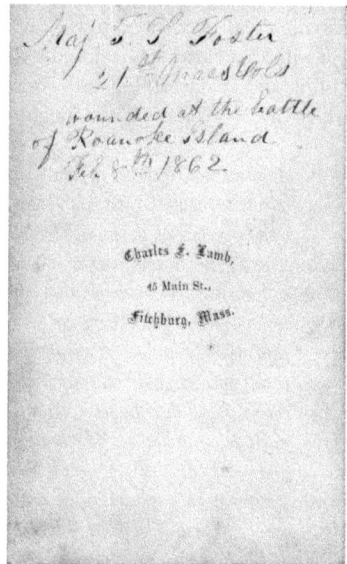

Left: Major Theodore Foster, 21st Massachusetts Infantry. *Right*: Back of Foster's image.

his actions during the Battle of Roanoke and staying on the line of battle for more than two hours after his wounding, Captain Foster was honored by his brother officers with a flag inscribed with the words, "The Officers of the 21st Regiment Massachusetts Volunteers to the brave Captain T.S. Foster, of Company D." This flag was later presented by Foster to the Fitchburg Public Library.[228]

The following month, on May 17, 1862, Theodore was promoted to major. The next note in his records referenced his absence from June 30, 1862, to September 8, 1862, when he was sick in Massachusetts. During this period, on September 2, 1862, Theodore was promoted again to lieutenant colonel. Though still suffering, Theodore was present for September/October and fought at South Mountain and Antietam, but he was not well, as he resigned on December 17, 1862.[229] In 1869, Theodore Foster joined the U.S. Customs Service and was working for it when he passed away suddenly while on duty on February 7, 1910. He was a senior inspector and eighty-three years old at the time of his passing. This death was marked by his comrades in the Military Order of the Loyal Legion, the Grand Army of the Republic and the Free Masons.[230] Lieutenant Colonel Theodore Foster is buried at Laurel Hill Cemetery, Fitchburg, Massachusetts.[231]

TAKEN IN FITCHBURG, MASSACHUSETTS, by photographer Charles F. Lamb, this CDV was likely made while Theodore Foster was on leave due to ill health in Massachusetts through the summer of 1862. The image was possibly a gift, as it has been signed with Foster's name, rank and regiment and even details his wounding on Roanoke Island in February 1862. As a bust shot, the image is dominated by Foster's dark-blue, double-breasted frock coat. The double row of seven evenly spaced buttons gives the coat away, as does its high collar and cuff buttons. The buttons down the front appear to be the general service large eagle buttons, six of which are visible in the left row, four in the right. There are also two small eagle buttons visible on Foster's right wrist. He has unbuttoned the fourth button in the right row to use as an impromptu pocket.

Major Foster's shoulder boards are both clearly visible in this image. Although the image is slightly washed out, the light-blue interior with gold embroidered borders are visible, as is a major's gold oak leaf symbol on the front of Foster's left shoulder board. Major Theodore Foster has completed his look with his magnificent mustache and small goatee, as well as by combing and likely oiling his hair.

17TH MICHIGAN INFANTRY

The 17th Michigan Infantry, known as the "Stonewall Regiment" for its action at Fox's Gap on South Mountain, was organized in Detroit, Michigan, beginning in the spring of 1862 and was mustered into the service of the United States on August 21, 1862. Six days later, the regiment started for Washington under command of Colonel William H. Withington. Upon its arrival, the 17th Michigan was assigned to the IX Army Corps, with which it remained for the extent of its service. Just over two weeks after shipping out for Washington, the boys of the Great Lake State were thrown into the Maryland Campaign. Heavily engaged at Fox's Gap, the regiment earned its nickname by driving Confederate troops from behind the stone walls near the Wise Farm.[232]

After proving itself in its baptism of fire on South Mountain, the 17th Michigan again fought hard at Antietam three days later. The regiment was fortunate to be in reserve at Fredericksburg in December 1862, but by March 1863, the 17th Michigan had been sent west to Kentucky. That June, the IX Corps aided in the Siege of Vicksburg. After this, it was ordered to help drive the Confederates from the Mississippi capital of Jackson before returning to Kentucky in August 1863. Made a part of the Army of the Ohio, the IX Corps took part in the East Tennessee Campaign in the fall of 1863 and defended Fort Sanders during the Confederate Siege of Knoxville in late November 1863. Returned to the Army of the Potomac in March 1864, the 17th Michigan was plunged into the Overland Campaign that spring. Engaged in battle repeatedly during this period, the 17th Michigan was near the Appomattox River during the winter of 1865 and ordered into Petersburg, Virginia, following the city's surrender on April 3, 1865, to act as the provost guard. On April 24, the 17th Michigan embarked at City Point for Alexandria, Virginia, and participated in the Grand Review in Washington on May 23, 1865. Mustered out on June 3, the regiment was shipped back to Michigan by train the following day. Arriving in Detroit on June 7, 1865, the 17th Michigan Infantry was paid and disbanded.[233]

Brigadier General Orlando Willcox, commander of the division the 17th Michigan was in, described the actions of the regiment in his official report:

> *In compliance with orders from General Reno, we left camp, 1 miles beyond Middletown, and marched to the base of South Mountain to support General Cox's division.—The attack was so sudden, the whole division being under this fire (a flank fire), that a temporary panic occurred until I caused the Seventy-ninth New York, Lieutenant-Colonel Morrison, and Seventeenth Michigan, Colonel Withington, on the extreme left, to draw across the road, facing the enemy, who were so close that we expected a charge to take Cook's battery. The Seventy-ninth and Seventeenth here deserve credit for their coolness and firmness in rallying and changing front under a heavy fire…*
>
> *I soon received orders from Generals Reno and McClellan to silence the enemy's battery at all hazards. Sent picket report to Reno, and was making disposition to charge, moving the Seventeenth Michigan so as to cross the hollow and flank the enemy's guns, when the enemy charged out of the woods on their side directly upon our front in a long, heavy line, extending beyond our left to Cox's right. I instantly gave the command "Forward," and we*

met them near the foot of the hill, the Forty-fifth Pennsylvania in front. The Seventeenth Michigan rushed down into the hollow, faced to the left, leaped over a stone fence, and took them in flank. Some of the supporting regiments over the slope of the hill fired over the heads of those in front, and after a severe contest of some minutes the enemy was repulsed, followed by our troops to the opposite slope and woods, forming their own position…

The Seventeenth Michigan, Colonel Withington, performed a feat that may vie with any recorded in the annals of war, and set an example to the oldest troops. This regiment had not been organized a single month, and was composed of raw levies.[234]

The Battle of South Mountain was the first battle fought by the 17th Michigan. Due to its fighting at Fox's Gap, the regiment reported losses of 26 enlisted killed, 4 officers and 102 enlisted wounded and no missing, for a total of 132.[235]

Among the wounded on South Mountain was First Sergeant Hiram Simpson. Simpson had mustered into Company K of the 17th Michigan on August 16, 1862, for three years of service as a sergeant. He stated that he was twenty-nine years old at the time and was paid a bounty of $25 plus a premium of $2 on his monthly pay. On September 13, 1862, Hiram was promoted to first sergeant, and the next day he was Wounded in Action at South Mountain.[236] His service records do not include any details as to his wound, but a *New York Times* article listing the casualties at South Mountain stated that he was wounded in the leg.[237] Due to this, Hiram was "absent" for November/December 1862. He returned to the regiment on January 16, 1863, and was "present" until October 31, 1863. Sergeant Simpson had apparently been "left sick [in] Laman Hospital, Knoxville October 20, 1863." Likely due to the needs of the regiment, he was demoted from first sergeant to sergeant on December 1, 1863. Hiram remained absent until February 29, 1864. After his return to the regiment, he was "present" for the rest of his service. Sergeant Simpson mustered out on June 3, 1865, having last been paid on December 31, 1864. Hiram had drawn $8.98 against his clothing allowance but was still due $75 in bounty money at the end of his service.[238] Although Hiram never filed for a pension, his mother did on November 17, 1884, according to his survivor's pension card.[239] Active in flower raising and display after the war, Hiram competed regularly in the Michigan State Fair.[240] Hiram Simpson died on September 3, 1873, in Adrian, Michigan, and is buried at Maple Grove Cemetery in Grass Lake, Michigan.[241]

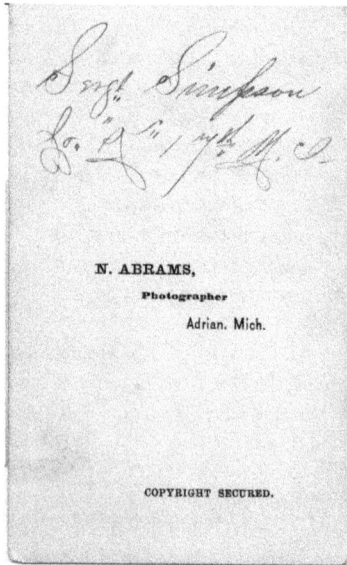

Left: First Sergeant Hiram Simpson, 17th Michigan Infantry. *Right*: Back of Simpson's image.

This bust image of Hiram Simpson was taken by photographer Noble Abrams out of Adrian, Michigan. The image was likely used as a calling card or gift by Simpson, as he has given his rank, name and regiment on the back. This image was either taken at the beginning of Simpson's enlistment, prior to his uniform being issued, or shortly after his service had ended, as the photographer left Adrian in 1867.[242] Regardless, his civilian sack coat, while comfortable, is a far cry from the uniform he wore at the beginning of his service. Musician David Lane of Company G described the uniform of the 17th Michigan prior to its going into action at South Mountain: "Dress coats buttoned up to the chin; upon our heads a high—crowned hat with a feather stuck jauntily on one side. White gloves in our pockets."[243] In uniform or not, Hiram Simpson has trimmed his beard and combed his hair to look his best for the image.

OF THESE SIX MEN who fought at Fox's Gap, five would be killed, wounded or have their constitutions destroyed by the war. Sergeant Simpson was wounded on slopes of South Mountain but recovered to serve out the rest of his enlistment. Lieutenant Colonel Foster was wounded prior to the Battle of South Mountain but recovered to fight there, although due to ill health he was forced to resign in the fall of 1862. Two of these men were later killed in action: Captain Gillis and Lieutenant Scudder, both in 1864. Captain Hohle was discharged for ill health, typhoid fever and diarrhea in July 1863, from which he died in September 1863, less than two months later. Finally, Corporal Hamilton was the lucky one, as he served out the war and returned to civilian life without having been wounded or reported sick during his service to his country.

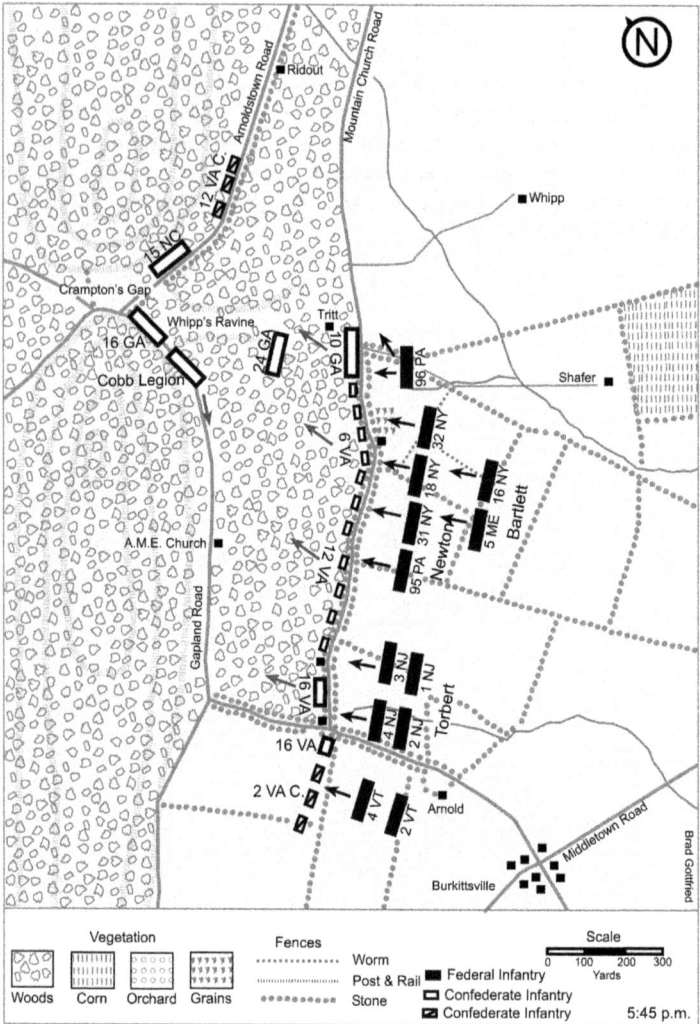

Map legend:

Vegetation: Woods, Corn, Orchard, Grains

Fences: Worm, Post & Rail, Stone

Scale: 0 100 200 300 Yards

Federal Infantry
Confederate Infantry
Confederate Infantry

5:45 p.m.

Map labels: Ridout, Mountain Church Road, Arnoldstown Road, 12 VAC, 15 NC, Crampton's Gap, 16 GA, Whipp's Ravine, 24 GA, Cobb Legion, 10 GA, Tritt, 96 PA, Whipp, Shafer, 6 VA, 32 NY, 18 NY, 16 NY, Bartlett, 5 ME, 31 NY, Newton, 95 PA, 12 VA, A.M.E. Church, Gapland Road, 16 VA, 3 NJ, 1 NJ, 4 NJ, 2 NJ, Torbert, 16 VA, 2 VA C., 4 VT, 2 VT, Arnold, Middletown Road, Burkittsville, Brad Gottfried

South Mountain—Crampton's Gap, 5:30 p.m.–5:45 p.m. *Map provided by Dr. Bradley Gottfried.*

Chapter 4

CRAMPTON'S GAP

W hile fighting raged to the north at Frosttown, Turner's and Fox's Gaps, the Union VI Corps, under command of Major General William B. Franklin, had been ordered to Rohrersville by way of Burkittsville and Crampton's Gap. Franklin was to cross South Mountain at Crampton's Gap and "cut off, destroy, or capture McLaws' command and relieve Colonel Miles," whose garrison at Harpers Ferry was still holding out on September 14. If General Franklin found the gap defended, he was ordered to attack vigorously a half hour after firing was heard coming from the fighting at the northern gaps.[244]

The map shows the dispositions of the opposing forces at about 5:30 p.m. On the left of the Union were two units from Brigadier General William Brooks's Vermont Brigade, protecting the left flank of the Federal line. In the lead was the 4th Vermont; in support was the 2nd Vermont. To the right of the Vermont units on the other side of the road was the 2nd New Jersey from Colonel Alfred Torbert's Brigade. The Federal troops to the right of the New Jersey men formed the brigade of Brigadier General John Newton. Deployed in line of battle, the first regiment in Newton's Brigade was the 95th Pennsylvania Infantry. To its right was the 31st New York Infantry, and holding the end of the brigade line was the 32nd New York Infantry. These units advanced toward a stone wall along Mountain Church Road, which runs along the base of South Mountain. By leaving Burkittsville following Gapland Road toward Crampton's Gap, the Vermont units were on the left. Turning right on Mountain Church Road passes along the Confederate battle line, with the Union infantry approaching over the open, rolling ground to the right.

4ᵀᴴ VERMONT INFANTRY

The 4th Vermont Infantry was raised in the summer of 1861 following the Union disaster at First Bull Run. The regiment was raised primarily from Bennington County, while also recruiting from Windsor, Orange, Orleans, Windham, Washington and Caledonia Counties.[245] The 4th Vermont was mustered into United States service for three years at Brattleboro, Vermont, on September 21, 1861, and immediately ordered to Washington. It was soon forwarded to Camp Advance, Virginia, where the regiment was united with the Vermont infantry regiments that made up the 1st Vermont Brigade. After suffering a difficult first winter in the service, the 4th Vermont and its comrades in the 1st Vermont Brigade were assigned to the VI Corps in the spring of 1862. The 4th Vermont served through the Peninsula Campaign, as well as the Maryland and Fredericksburg Campaigns in 1862. Following the "Mud March" and wintering near Falmouth, Virginia, the regiment took part in the 1863 Chancellorsville, Gettysburg and Mine Run Campaigns and helped quell the draft rights in New York City that summer. The spring of 1864 brought the Overland Campaign, followed by opening of the Siege of Petersburg and the Shenandoah Valley Campaign.[246] The 4th Vermont remained with the VI Corps throughout its long service and fought its last battle on April 6, 1865, at Sailor's Creek, just days before the surrender at Appomattox. The regiment participated in the various reviews of Vermont troops in June, and on July 13, 1865, the 4th Vermont Infantry mustered out of Federal service.[247]

During the afternoon fighting on September 14, 1862, for Crampton's Gap in South Mountain, the actions of the 4th Vermont were remarked on by its brigade commander, Brigadier General William Brooks, in his report:

> *As soon as the nature of the ground and the exact position of the wall could be determined, the Fourth Vermont, Lieutenant-Colonel Stoughton, was deployed with the Second Vermont, under Major Walbridge, in support in second line, and the other three regiments in support on the edge of the town. In this position an advance was made against the wall, which was carried immediately, and some 15 or 20 prisoners captured. The advance was continued by the Fourth and Second without further opposition, until the top of the mountain was reached, when the Fourth was ordered to take the crest to our left, toward the battery that fired upon us as we passed through the town.*[248]

At South Mountain, the 4th Vermont did not report the strength of the regiment. Its losses, however, were recorded as one enlisted man killed, ten wounded and none missing, for a total of eleven. No casualties occurred among the officers during the fighting for Crampton's Gap.[249]

Among those serving in Company D of the 4th Vermont Infantry on September 14, 1862, was Sergeant Joseph P. Aikens. Upon his enlistment, Joseph stated that he was from Barnard, Vermont, and twenty-four years old. In the company descriptive book, Joseph was described as five feet, five and a half inches tall, with a light complexion, blue eyes and light hair. He was a farmer before the war. Joseph mustered in as a private on September 21, 1861, having previously served in the 1st Vermont Infantry, a three-month regiment, at the beginning of the war. His service records showed him as "present" after December 31, 1861, by which time he had been promoted to corporal. On April 1, 1862, Joseph was again promoted, to sergeant, and shown as "present" for September/October 1862, so he was at Crampton's Gap with his regiment. Sergeant Aikens was promoted to first sergeant on January 1, 1863, with a note that he had been "paid as 3rd Sergt. to Octo 31st." On December 15, 1863, Joseph reenlisted, and it was noted in his records that he had drawn on October 1, $18.91 against his clothing allowance, meaning he owed the government for the additional supplies. Sometime in January or February 1864, Joseph was reported as "Absent Sick in camp near Brandy Station." When he returned is not clear, but in May he was transferred to Company C by reason of promotion. That report also noted that Sergeant Aikens was "due $7.00 as 1st Sergt. from Jany 5 to Feb 15, 1864." On May 5, Joseph was promoted to first lieutenant. His final promotion came on August 9, 1864, when he was made captain of Company A. Joseph was "present" until October 19, 1864, when he was wounded at the Battle of Cedar Creek, Virginia. The wound was in the left thigh and resulted in his discharge on March 3, 1865.[250] After the war, Joseph lived in Windsor, Vermont, and passed away on February 9, 1924. He is buried at Hartford Point Cemetery, Hartford, Vermont.[251]

THE IMAGE OF JOSEPH Aikens was taken some time after his promotion to first sergeant on January 1, 1863. While there is no back mark to give clues as to where the image was taken, it is possible the sergeant waited until his veterans' furlough to have the image made. Joseph Aikens was one of 210 members of the 4th Vermont who reenlisted in 1864 for the duration of the war. Those veterans received their furlough home during the winter of

Left: Sergeant Joseph P. Aikens, 4th Vermont Infantry. *Right*: Back of Aiken's image.

1864, prior to the opening of the Overland Campaign.[252] As Joseph signed the back of the image, as well as gave his regiment and rank, it is likely that this was either a gift or used as a calling card by the sergeant.

The image was taken in a studio using a nondescript background, likely a pulldown as it does not go all the way to the floor. The photographer also provided a chair for Joseph Aikens to sit in, as well as a covered table and a tasseled drape for decoration. Just behind Joseph, a brace is partially hidden by the spindles of his chair.

Though he is seated, the vast majority of Sergeant Aikens's uniform can still be made out. Starting with his shoes, Joseph appears to be wearing the basic government-issued footwear, which was known by several names, including "brogans" or "Jefferson bootees." These were a basic leather shoe with leather soles and heels, mass-produced in the Union with the rough side out and tied with leather laces.[253] Sitting with his legs crossed, Joseph's trousers are the sky blue of the volunteers, but interestingly, they lack the inch-and-a-half-wide dark-blue stripe down the seam that denotes his rank of sergeant.[254]

There is no lack of rank, however, on his frock coat, with the light-blue sergeant's chevrons and diamond of a first sergeant clearly visible. The chevron's color is specific to each branch of service; in this case, the light blue is for the infantry.[255] This is also reflected in the light- or sky blue piping near his right cuff, as well as at the collar of the frock. The frock coat itself is dark blue and skirted, with nine large eagle buttons running down the front, eight of which can be seen in this image, as well as two small eagle buttons on each wrist. Likely for comfort, Joseph has left his top four buttons undone, allowing for a good view of his plaid cravat, a private purchase that was not a required piece of the enlisted uniform. The collar of a freshly starched shirt or a shirt with a new paper collar can just be seen under Joseph's jawline.

To finish off the image, Joseph Aikens is wearing his forage cap, with its distinctive flopped appearance. With well over 4 million of these caps produced by the Federal government or purchased for Union forces, there was a wide variety in shape and style. All were made with dark-blue jean cloth, leather bill and chin strap with two small eagle buttons.[256] As for Joseph himself, his hair is relatively short, and his mustache neatly trimmed, per regulations.[257]

2ND VERMONT INFANTRY

The first of Vermont's three-year regiments, the 2nd Vermont Infantry was raised from across the state and organized at Burlington prior to being mustered into United States service on June 20, 1861.[258] The regiment left the state four days later for Washington and encamped on Capital Hill until July 10. The 2nd Vermont was assigned to Heintzelman's Division and fought with that command at the First Battle of Bull Run. That September, the 2nd Vermont was combined with the 3rd, 4th, 5th and later the 6th Vermont Infantries to form the 1st Vermont Brigade. This brigade was attached to the VI Corps in the spring of 1862 and fought with that corps for the duration of the war. Over the course of its service, the 2nd Vermont, with the rest of the Vermont Brigade and VI Corps, served primarily with the Army of the Potomac, taking part in all of its major campaigns, and also with the Army of the Shenandoah in the summer and fall of 1864. Those of the 2nd Vermont who did not reenlist were mustered out of service in June 1864, while the veteran volunteers and recruits continued through the 1864 Shenandoah Valley Campaign before returning to the Army of the Potomac at Petersburg, Virginia. The 2nd Vermont participated in the breakthrough at Petersburg on April 2, 1865, forcing the opening of the final campaign of the war in the east and fought its last battle at Sailor's Creek on April 6, 1865.[259] In June, the 2nd Vermont and comrades marched in multiple reviews and on July 15, 1865, mustered out of service.[260]

At South Mountain, the actions of the 2nd Vermont were described in its regimental history as follows: "At about 5:30 P.M. as Bartlett was about to move his brigade forward, the two New Jersey regiments on Torbert's far left jumped the gun and ran toward the base of the mountain.—With their battle lines formed and bayonets fixed, the Vermonters charged at the double-quick simultaneously with the Jerseymen on the right, charging square into the 2nd Virginia Cavalry and the 16th Virginia Infantry firing from behind their stone wall.—After jumping over the stone wall, the Vermonters headed west."[261]

Being in a supporting position, the 2nd Vermont was fortunate to suffer few casualties during the struggle for Crampton's Gap. The 2nd Vermont reported losses of zero killed, five wounded and zero missing, for a total of five.[262]

Among those fortunate soldiers was Francis M. Edgerton. Edgerton mustered into Company B of the 2nd Vermont on June 20, 1861, for three years as a sergeant. He stated he was twenty-one and a student in Castleton, Vermont, before joining the unit. The company descriptive book notes that Francis was five feet, nine and a half inches tall, with a light complexion, blue eyes and brown hair; he was born in Poultney, Vermont, on April 11, 1840. His service records show he was "present" from muster in, until the November/December 1862 period. On September 18, 1861, he was detailed as adjutant clerk, and he was promoted to sergeant major on October 14, 1861. After the turn of the year on January 24, 1862, Francis was promoted again, to second lieutenant in Company F, and shortly thereafter detailed as provost marshal until sometime in July. On August 4, 1862, he was promoted again, to adjutant and first lieutenant. Following the fighting at Crampton's Gap, Francis was reassigned to Brigadier General Albion P. Howe's staff as "AAAG," or acting assistant adjutant general, on November 2, 1862. Though briefly returned to his unit, he was again detached to General Howe's staff in March/April 1863. Francis remained with General Howe until his muster out on June 29, 1864, almost exactly three years after his muster-in date.[263] Francis passed away on December 17, 1907, and was buried at East Poultney Cemetery in Poultney, Vermont.[264]

Left: First Lieutenant Francis M. Edgerton, 2nd Vermont Infantry. *Right*: Back of Edgerton's image.

IT IS INTERESTING THAT the photograph of Francis Edgerton was taken in Hagerstown, Maryland, just ten miles north of Sharpsburg and the Antietam battlefield. In the published letters of Private D.D. Priest, also of the 2nd Vermont, he wrote from Hagerstown on September 27 and October 17, 19 and 28.[265] General Brooks's Brigade of the VI Corps was stationed in Hagerstown by October 1862, making it likely that Francis had his photograph taken by Elias M. Recher at that time.[266] The photo itself was apparently a gift or calling card, as Francis signed it and provided his rank and regiment.

The photograph of Lieutenant Francis Edgerton has a number of trappings and decorations, including a column atop a large pedestal for the subject to lean against, as well as drapery. A brace was also provided for Lieutenant Edgerton, the feet of which can be seen behind him.

As for the lieutenant himself, he is wearing his officer's uniform for the photo. Unlike the enlisted men of the 2nd Vermont, Francis was responsible for obtaining his own uniform.[267] Starting at his footwear, these appear to be a little nicer than the standard-issued shoe, as the light is picking up their shine. Officers were permitted to wear boots if they wished, and it is possible that these, with their tapering toe, are officer's boots.[268] An ankle boot or a nicer shoe is just as possible, however, as having worked his way up from the ranks, Francis may have opted for lighter footwear.

It should be noted that Francis Edgerton is wearing the early war dark-blue officer's trousers with light- or sky blue piping running down the seam to designate the infantry branch of service.[269] This particular style was superseded in December 1861 by General Orders No. 108, which allowed for sky blue kersey wool trousers to be worn by both officers and enlisted men.[270] Although the light-blue pants and dark-blue coats would become the iconic look of Union soldiers in the Civil War, many officers and the enlisted of the Regular Army retained their dark-blue trousers for as long as they could to better differentiate themselves from the volunteer forces.

Dominating the photograph of Francis Edgerton is his frock coat. Cut for an officer, Francis's dark-blue frock has a longer skirt, coming almost to the knee, and is much fuller in the sleeves than the enlisted man's frock would be.[271] In addition, there are three small eagle buttons that can be seen near his left cuff, as opposed to two cuff buttons seen on enlisted frocks, along with the nine large eagle buttons running down the front of the coat. Unlike the general service eagle buttons used by the enlisted, the eagle buttons on an officer's frock would have the branch of service indicated on them by a letter found on the shield in front of the eagle—in this case an "I" for the infantry.[272]

On each of Lieutenant Edgerton's shoulders are his shoulder boards; the boards are gold embroidered and have a single gold bar at each end, indicating a first lieutenant. It is interesting to note how dark the interior of his shoulder boards are and that they are apparently the same color as the frock coat. As an infantry officer, these should be light blue, but as Francis had been assigned to an officer's staff, his shoulder boards are the dark blue meant for staff positions.[273]

A crisp white shirt is peeking out from his low collar, likely a new paper collar for the photo. Francis Edgerton completed his attire by wearing his officer's cap. It is difficult to tell if this cap is a kepi, cut more in the style of the French, or an officer's forage cap. Regardless, Francis has followed regulations by having an embroidered gold hunter's horn, signifying the infantry, placed on the front of the cap. It is hard to tell from this image, but he may have included a silver "2" within the loop of the horn, for the 2nd Vermont Infantry.[274] The chin strap and slide buckle of the cap can also be made out in this photograph. To finish off his look, Francis has trimmed his beard and combed his hair for the image.

2ND NEW JERSEY INFANTRY

The 2nd New Jersey Infantry was organized and equipped by May 18, 1861. Eight days later, the regiment was mustered into the service of the United States for three years at Camp Olden, Trenton, New Jersey. It left the state on June 28 with 38 officers and 1,006 men. The 2nd New Jersey was assigned to the New Jersey Brigade with its sister regiments, the 1st, 3rd and 4th Infantries. Reenlisting in 1863, the regiment served for the remainder of the war and mustered out at Hall's Hill, Virginia, on July 11, 1865, having taken part in all the fighting and marching resulting in the surrender of Lee at Appomattox.[275]

Colonel Samuel Buck, the commanding officer of the regiment, wrote in his official report of Crampton's Gap:

> [A]*dvanced by the flank under cover of rising ground until within musket-range of the enemy; formed in line of battle (having the left of the advance line of the brigade), and moved forward to relieve one regiment of Bartlett's brigade, posted in rear of a rail fence. We occupied the same position which they had left, and opened fire on the enemy. After firing about twenty minutes, the Fourth Regiment of the second line advanced through our lines and made a charge across an open field, followed immediately by us, both reaching the stone fence about the same time, behind which the enemy were in position. The enemy broke and fled, we pursuing them up the hill and through the pass. As we advanced, the regiment wheeled to the right, the left resting on the crest of the hill on the left of the road.*[276]

Due to the fighting at Crampton's Gap in South Mountain, the 2nd New Jersey reported losses of ten enlisted killed, one officer and forty-four enlisted wounded and zero missing, for a total of fifty-five.[277]

Charging with the 2nd New Jersey was Private Andrew G. Wintermute. Andrew mustered into Company B on May 27, 1861. He did not list a residence, although the Sussex, New Jersey county history states that he was from Stillwater.[278] When Andrew mustered at Trenton for a three-year enlistment, he gave his age as twenty-one. His service records show that he was "not present" through the rest of 1861. Private Wintermute was "present" from January/February 1862 for the rest of his service. The first note in Andrew's records was for the September/October 1862 period, when he owed the sutler payment ("due sutler $1.00"), although the reason is not explained. On December 25, 1862, Andrew was promoted to corporal. He was promoted again on April 20, 1863, to sergeant shortly after his return from a ten-day furlough on April 3. When Andrew had served his three years, he mustered out at Newark on June 21, 1864. Andrew had last been paid on February 29, 1864.[279] Andrew Wintermute filed for a pension on July 6, 1885, which was granted following his death in Pomona, California, on February 16, 1897.[280] After this, his wife received a pension.[281]

PICTURED HERE WITH HIS corporal's stripes, Andrew Wintermute likely had this photograph taken in April 1863 when he was home on leave. His image taken in Newton, New Jersey, by photographer I.G. Owen, Andrew probably presented this photo as a gift for a friend or family member back home or a comrade in the ranks. He signed the back of the image, which has its own decoration of the Union eagle: "Wintermute, Andrew G. Co B 2nd Regt N.J. Vols."

Taken in a standing pose, the image shows that Andrew Wintermute's uniform is a great representation of the uniforms having two sizes, either too big or too small.[282] In this case, both his pants and coat appear to be quite large. The picture itself was taken in the Owen Studio using a particularly beat-up chair on which Andrew placed his unadorned, square-billed forage cap. The cap's leather chin strap with brass slide buckle and the two small eagle buttons that hold that strap on are visible. The studio also provided a brace, which can be seen just behind Andrew's feet. On his feet are blackened leather shoes or bootees; these would have been provided by the government, and under ideal circumstances, the enlisted soldier would be issued four pairs of shoes per year.[283]

Moving up from his shoes, Andrew is wearing a pair of light-blue wool pants indicative of the volunteers. As mentioned, these seem quite large on him, and looking at the waistline, there is a large button helping keep his pants in place. This is likely a repair job, as the buttons on Federal trousers are small tin buttons,[284] whereas this appears as large as a coat button. The rest of the buttons for the fly are under a fold on the pants. Just above the waistline, there is also a glimpse of Andrew's shirt. As the issued flannel shirt was considered an undergarment, it was not supposed to be seen in polite company without a vest or something else covering it.[285] Andrew Wintermute does not apparently have a vest and so has conformed to regulation by having his frock coat buttoned at the neck for modesty, while still being mostly open for ventilation.[286]

The frock, with its nine buttons all visible, as well as the long skirting around the waist, is very large, and on both sleeves can be seen the light-blue

Left: Private Andrew G. Wintermute, 2nd New Jersey Infantry. *Right*: Back of Wintermute's image.

chevrons of an infantry corporal. The two cuff buttons on the left sleeve can also be seen. Finally, a very faint light-blue piping, also signifying the infantry, can be made out on the left sleeve, as well as around the collar of the frock.[28] The coat's high collar blocks any further details around the neck. As per regulations, Andrew Wintermute trimmed his mustache and combed his hair, the shine suggesting he may have applied some sort of pomade prior to the picture being taken.

95TH PENNSYLVANIA INFANTRY

Much of the 95th Pennsylvania Volunteer Infantry had been raised from Philadelphia and its immediate area, besides one company, which had been recruited in Burlington County, New Jersey. These men, many of whom had experience with the militia or had already served in the three-month regiments, enlisted for three years of service. The companies of the regiment were mustered into service from August 23 to October 16, 1861. The 95th Pennsylvania was present in all the major campaigns of the Army of the Potomac. The regiment's last engagement was the Battle of Sailor's Creek during the Appomattox Campaign. Afterward, it moved to Danville, Virginia, and then to Richmond, finally returning to Washington to muster out on July 17, 1865.[288]

During the 1862 Maryland Campaign, the 95th Pennsylvania was commanded by Colonel Gustavus W. Town. In his after-action report, Town described how the regiment upon entering Burkittsville came under fire from both Confederate artillery and skirmishers before deploying into line of battle. The regiment moved up in support of the 31st New York Volunteers but was soon ordered to the right:

> We then received orders from Brig. Gen. Newton in person to march by flank toward the right, and under his direction, charged up the mountain, reaching the road near its crest. At this time, we were on a line with the most advanced of our troops, and received orders to continue the charge out the main road across the mountain. Advancing in line of battle, the wings extending to the right and left of the road, we were soon joined on the left by a portion of the First New Jersey Brigade, under command of Col. Torbert. The enemy being here in line to oppose our farther progress, we attacked them immediately, driving them from their position and sending a number of prisoners to the rear. Continuing the pursuit close upon them, they made another stand, but were again driven from it. Halting for a few moments to reform line of battle, in connection with the New Jersey troops upon our left, we again advanced to attack the enemy, who were hoping to reform to protect their wagon train, then in sight of us. To assist this endeavor, they had placed a battery in position on the road, which opened upon our line with canister immediately upon our advancing. The line recoiled but for a moment, and then, with shouts, charged upon it, firing as it advanced, the shots being directed by the flash of the artillery, as it was now too dark to distinguish the gunners at that distance.
>
> Here orders were brought to us by Col. Bartlett in person to halt, it being then dark, and retire to the woods at the foot of the mountain, and take up position until further orders.[289]

Colonel Town ended his report stating, "Casualties 1 killed, 13, wounded and 1 missing, total 15."[290]

Swept up in the advance of the 95th Pennsylvania Infantry was William J. Campbell of Philadelphia (although another source has him being born in

Ireland[291]), a member of Company A. Prior to his service in the 95th Pennsylvania, William had enlisted as a private on April 24, 1861, with the 18th Pennsylvania Infantry for three months. He mustered out on August 7. Two weeks later, on August 21, 1861, William joined Company A of the 95th Pennsylvania Infantry, mustering in as a private for three years of service. Possibly due to his previous experience, on October 24, 1861, Campbell was promoted to commissary sergeant. The following year, on July 21, 1862, Sergeant Campbell was promoted again to sergeant major, the highest-ranking noncommissioned officer in the regiment and the official go-between for the enlisted men and the regimental officers. William Campbell was the 95th Pennsylvania's sergeant major at the Battle of South Mountain less than two months later. Though unscathed at the fighting at Crampton's Gap or Antietam three days later, William was wounded on December 13, 1862, at the Battle of Fredericksburg. The wound must not have been serious, as William was not reported at any hospital and was listed as "present" during this period. On February 10, 1863, William was promoted to regimental quartermaster and commissioned a first lieutenant. The following December, Lieutenant Campbell was on ten days of leave granted on December 17, 1863, with a note in his records that he was to be paid at "1/2 pay" while on leave. This occurred again when William went on leave March 5, 1864. The report for July/August 1864 shows Lieutenant Campbell on detached duty in the division Quartermaster Department. On November 2, 1864, William mustered out of the army.[292] Although he did not reenlist during the Civil War, William Campbell's service to his country was not over. He joined the 22nd United States Infantry on May 21, 1867, as a second lieutenant. He was promoted back to first lieutenant on May 12, 1875, and died on December 17, 1886.

THIS STANDING IMAGE OF William Campbell was taken in the Philadelphia studio of photographer F. Gutekunst. Campbell signed the back of the photograph, "Very truly yours Wm J Campbell Lt R.Q.M. 95th P.V." This inscription suggests that the photograph was given as a gift, but it is also one of several clues that helps identify roughly when this image was taken. As William identified himself as both a lieutenant and the regimental quartermaster, this photo was taken after his promotion to that rank and position in February 1863. The studio this image was taken in was located in Philadelphia, so Campbell would have been on leave to have this taken, narrowing the potential date to December 1863 or March 1864. However, the biggest clue is the green three-cent tax stamp. The three-cent stamps

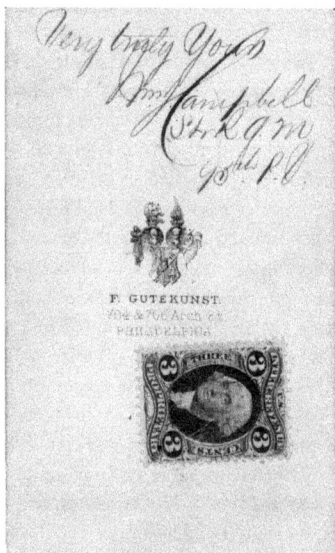

Left: Sergeant Major William J. Campbell, 95th Pennsylvania Infantry. *Right*: Back of Campbell's image.

were for images that cost less than fifty cents. Begun in August 1864, the tax continued for two years before being repealed in August 1866.[293] As such, this photograph of William Campbell was most likely taken in November 1864, just after he mustered out of the 95th Pennsylvania Infantry.

The image shows Lieutenant William Campbell standing leisurely, with his arm resting on a decorative baluster and his hand in his pocket. He is wearing a clean pair of private purchase shoes, as well as a dark-blue pair of officer's trousers. The eighth-of-an-inch sky blue welt or piping, signifying the infantry, can be seen running up the outer seam of his left leg. At his waist starts his dark-blue vest; five buttons (possible Federal eagles) are visible due to his coat being partially open. Just above the fifth vest button from the bottom can be seen some sort of tie or decorative line. This is possibly a watch line attached to the buttonhole or perhaps a simple fix for a missing button.

Over William Campbell's vest, open except for a single button at the collar, is his coat. Dark blue, with a short standing collar and large closely spaced buttons, this appears to be an officer's frock coat. Four of the buttons are easily seen, with a fifth just peeking out from under the overcoat. There are also eight buttonholes opposite that can be seen, suggesting the nine-button pattern of a frock, although no indication of the skirting is visible. The other option is that this coat could be either a frock that has had the skirt removed or perhaps an officer's shell jacket, also known as a roundabout. Rarer in the infantry than in the mounted arms of the service, the shell jacket was buttoned to the waist with between eight and twelve buttons.[294]

The overcoat that dominates William Campbell's image appears to be a modified version of the cloak coat. These dark-blue overcoats were the original officer's overcoat, traditionally closed with four loops of black silk cord. This coat, however, has four buttons that can be seen, with a fifth likely being covered by a fold. The cloak coat used a black silk braid to bind its edges, as well as display rank on the sleeves, with the braid forming one to five knots depending on the rank. This coat was a direct copy of the 1845 French design and had a long, heavy cape, which can be seen here, that reached the sleeves. It is interesting to see the cloak coat in a later war image, as General Orders No. 102 from November 1861 stated, "In time of actual field service, officers of Cavalry, Artillery, and Infantry are permitted to wear the light blue overcoat prescribed for enlisted men of the mounted corps."[295] The enlisted man's greatcoat would have been far cheaper to procure than this modified cloak coat. William Campbell was either sparing no expense or perhaps wearing a prop provided by the photo gallery.

To look his best, William Campbell has on either a freshly starched shirt or a new paper collar that is poking up from his coat collar. He has chosen not to wear a cravat for this image, although as an officer he should be according to the regulations.[296] His facial hair has been trimmed, and on his head sits an officer's slouch hat. This was a soft, usually felt, hat with a wide brim that was worn for comfort by both officers and enlisted men, particularly those soldiers in the Western Theater.[297] Decorating the hat is what appears to be a hat cord encircling the base of the crown. Though difficult to make out, the hat cord should be black silk with gold for any officer.[298] Finally, Campbell has also included the regulation infantry patch on the front, the hunter's horn on a black patch.

31ST NEW YORK INFANTRY

The 31st New York Infantry was known as the "Montezuma Regiment" due to a large part of the men having been recruited by Lieutenant Colonel

William H. Browne, a veteran of the Mexican-American War. The regiment was raised primarily in New York City but contained one company from Williamsburg. The 31st New York completed its mustering into service on June 13, 1861, at Riker's Island and left the state for Washington on June 24. A month later, the Montezuma regiment fought at First Bull Run and was placed in Franklin's Division that fall. In the spring of 1862, the 31st New York became part of VI Corps, with which it fought during the Seven Days, as well as the Maryland and Fredericksburg Campaigns. They went into winter quarters at White Oak Church, Virginia, only to have to participate in the failed Mud March in January 1863. Being one of New York's two-year regiments, the 31st New York's last campaign was in early May 1863 at Chancellorsville, where it suffered significant casualties at Second Fredericksburg. Its term of enlistment expiring, the regiment returned to its old camp on Riker's Island until May 21, 1863. From there, the 31st New York left for New York City and was mustered out on June 4, 1863. Those men who had enlisted for three years were transferred to the 121st New York Infantry at that time.[299]

At Crampton's Gap, the 31st New York was commanded by the lieutenant colonel of the 32nd New York, Francis E. Pinto, who wrote in his after-action report of Crampton's Gap:

> *I was ordered to deploy my regiment in line of battle on the left of the Thirty-second Regiment New York State Volunteers, which placed me on the extreme left of the storming force, and advanced to the attack. The regiment advanced in good order, notwithstanding the numerous fences in their way, and the heavy fire of shell and musketry had no effect to disorder my line.*
>
> *I took up position on the left of the Sixteenth Regiment New York Volunteers, skirmishers of the Twenty-seventh Regiment New York Volunteers falling back to the rear, who were receiving a heavy fire from the enemy, concealed behind a stone wall on the road and barn back of the road. I remained in this position until I saw the troops on my right moving forward, when I instantly gave the order to charge, which was promptly obeyed by jumping a fence and passing through a corn-field with an unearthly yell. The enemy before us broke and fled right and left.*[300]

The fighting at Crampton's Gap did not cost the 31st New York greatly. Regimental losses were reported as one killed, three wounded and zero missing, for a total of four.[301]

On September 8, 1862, just before the Battle of South Mountain, Second Lieutenant Erskine Rich, a veteran of the famous 84th New York Infantry, also known as the 14th Brooklyn Militia, mustered into Company I of the 31st New York. Rich's original enlistment with the 84th New York had begun when he mustered into Company H on September 13, 1861, for the duration of the war. Enlisting in New York City, he stated he was twenty years old at the time. The company descriptive book describes Erskine as five feet, seven inches tall, with a light complexion, blue eyes and light hair; he was working as a clerk in Brooklyn. Less than two months into his service, Rich was captured on November 18, 1861, while on outpost duty. Sent to Richmond, Virginia, Rich was exchanged on February 19, 1862, and returned to the unit. He was listed as "present" from then until September 8, 1862, when he was listed as a "deserter."[302]

In actuality, Erskine had taken a promotion and mustered into Company I of the 31st New York Infantry on that date. It seems that his original unit did not get the word of his advancement for some time, as he was listed as a deserter through April 1864. Now with the 31st New York Infantry, Lieutenant Rich was "present" through May 2, 1863, having been promoted to first lieutenant on January 19 of that year. On May 4, Erskine was again taken prisoner following the fighting near Salem Church during the Chancellorsville Campaign. Sent to Richmond on May 9, he was paroled at City Point on May 15. Shortly thereafter, Lieutenant Rich was mustered out on June 4, 1863, in New York City, as the two-year term of the 31st New York had expired.[303] However, Erskine's service to his country was not over, as he reenlisted on January 22, 1864, and was commissioned a first lieutenant, this time in the 39th New York Infantry. Erskine was Wounded in Action on May 12, 1864, at Spotsylvania Court House. He was promoted to captain of Company F on December 31, 1864, and mustered out with his company on July 1, 1865, in Alexandria, Virginia.[304] After the war, Erskine returned to Brooklyn and worked as a city weigher. He applied for and received a pension for his military service in 1899. He applied for an increase in his pension due to multiple medical issues in the early twentieth century but was repeatedly denied. Erskine Rich passed away in 1905 and is buried at Green Wood Cemetery, Brooklyn, New York, Section 43, Lot 212.[305]

LIEUTENANT ERSKINE RICH PROVIDED not only his name, rank and regiment on the back of this image but also the likely date the photograph was taken, May 28, 1863. If that date is the date of the image, then this photo was

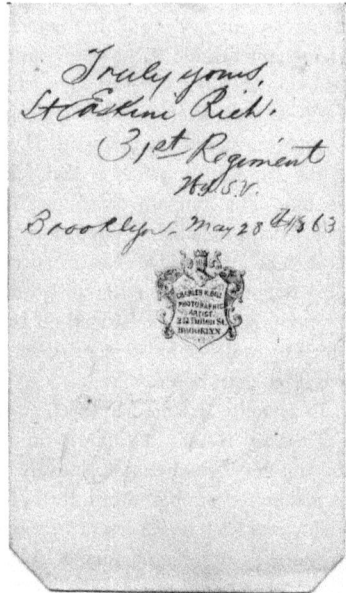

Left: Second Lieutenant Erskine Rich, 31st New York Infantry. *Right*: Back of Rich's image.

taken at the Charles K. Ball Studio in Brooklyn, New York, just days before the 31st New York mustered out of the service. In many ways, this image can be thought of as a senior or graduate portrait, and like with graduates today, this CDV was likely given as a gift, as Rich wrote "Truly yours" as part of his inscription on the back.

The Ball Studio provided the classic column on a pedestal for Lieutenant Rich to lean against, as well as a brace to keep his head still, the feet of which can just barely be seen behind him. On Erskine's feet are private purchase leather shoes. Nicer than the rough issued shoe for the enlisted, these appear to have the smooth side out and are slightly polished. His trousers are the dark-blue pants of an officer, with an eighth-inch light-blue piping, indicating the infantry, running up the seams. In this image, the piping can be seen on the outside of his left leg.

Beginning just above the knee is the skirting of Lieutenant Rich's long dark-blue frock coat. Looking closely, there appears to be some minor damage to the unhemmed skirting on the frock, just above the right knee.

What is particularly unique about this frock coat are the eight visible buttons running down the front. They do not appear to be the large Federal eagle buttons but instead are New York state seal buttons. The bulbous design with prominent ring can be seen, while the button itself has the state seal as well as the state motto "Excelsior" printed along the bottom edge.[306] Eight of the nine buttons are visible on the front of the coat; the ninth is likely under the lieutenant's sword belt and sash. There are also three small New York state seal buttons that can be seen running along the cuff. These buttons may have been available with the coat when it was purchased, or Erskine may have purchased them separately. Also featured prominently on the frock are the shoulder boards, which have been washed out in the photo but would have had the single gold bar on each end designating a first lieutenant.

Another indicator of Lieutenant Erskine Rich's rank is the sash and sword belt around his waist. For an infantry officer, the sash was to be silk net and crimson in color. It was also worn over the coat whenever the officer was on duty, including combat, except for when on stable or fatigue duty. The sash had silk bullion fringe ends, which can be seen beneath Erskine's left hand, and was wrapped twice around the waist and tied behind the left hip.[307] The sash fringes here have been draped over the sword belt and are forward on the left hip, likely as further decoration for the image. The sword belt itself is based on the 1851 Model. This black leather belt was 1.5 to 2 inches wide and closed with a rectangular belt plate. This belt would have also had slings to help carry the weight of the officer's sword. The over-the-shoulder sling can be seen here with its brass buckles.[308] Lieutenant Rich's belt plate is likely the 2-inch-wide Model 1851 plate. These were made of brass and had a raised rim. Featured on the plate itself was a spread eagle, which can just be made out in this image. Beneath the eagle was a separately affixed silver wreath, while above the national bird was a scroll inscribed with the motto "E PLURIBUS UNUM."[309]

Cradled in Lieutenant Erskine Rich's left arm is his sword. The sword was not only a symbol of rank but also a required piece of equipment when on duty.[310] The lieutenant obviously wanted the blade, normally seen hanging on the left hip, featured in his image. The sword is a Model 1850 foot officer's sword. It features a wire-wrapped fish skin grip with a branch guard that expands to an oval counter guard. Though impossible to tell at this angle, the guards of these swords could feature a wide variety of natural or patriotic decorations. Leaves, scrolls and patriotic emblems were all very common. The pommel is attached to the guard branch and has a Phrygian helmet design. The scabbard of this weapon has three brass fittings. The first is known as the throat, which is at Lieutenant Rich's elbow and features one of the brass rings used to attach the scabbard to the sword belt. The second fitting is covered and about where the lieutenant's hand is—it has the second ring. The final fitting is the long brass finial at the end of the scabbard called the drag. The blade itself was etched, often with laurels or other patriotic emblems varying widely from maker to maker.[311] The lieutenant's final touch is the sword knot attached to the guard branch of his sword. Meant to help keep the user from completely losing his blade in the event he had it knocked from his hand, an officer's sword knot was a gold lace strap with gold bullion tassel.[312]

Lieutenant Rich's high collar, as well as the shadow, hides whether or not he is wearing a cravat, but he has made an effort to look as professional as possible for the image. Beyond having nearly the full extent of his uniform in frame, although curiously he did not include his hat, the lieutenant has finished off his look by combing his hair, sweeping it forward above the ears.

32ND NEW YORK INFANTRY

The 32nd New York Infantry was called the 1st California regiment by its original colonel, Roderic Matheson, a Scottish-born New Yorker who had moved to California during the gold rush and had become influential in California politics. The 32nd New York was mustered into United States service for two years on May 31, 1861, on Staten Island and left the state for Washington on June 29, 1861. During its service, the regiment fought in the campaigns of the Army of the Potomac through the spring of 1863. Its term of service expiring, the regiment returned on May 8, 1863, to Belle Plain, and on the twenty-fifth the three-years men were transferred to the 121st New York Infantry. The rest of the 32nd New York mustered out on June 9, 1863.[313]

Tragically, both Colonel Matheson and Major George Lemon were mortally wounded at the Crampton's Gap fighting during the Battle of South Mountain. With Lieutenant Colonel Francis E. Pinto temporarily commanding the 31st New York, there was apparently no one to write the after-action report for the regiment. Their actions and those of their comrades were remarked on by their brigade commander, Brigadier General John Newton (emphasis added):

> *The troops were under a very severe fire from the enemy's musketry and artillery, they (the enemy) being covered by woods, stone walls, ledges of rock, &c.*

Crampton's Gap

After a fusillade of about one hour and a half, with but little impression being made upon the enemy, the order to charge was given, in which the entire infantry of the division, with the exception of the One hundred and twenty-first New York Volunteers, were engaged. The charge was short and decisive, and the enemy was driven from his stronghold in a very few moments, although our loss was severe in accomplishing this object. The Eighteenth and Thirty-second New York on the right of our line, aided by other regiments of the division, charged up the almost inaccessible mountain to its summit, driving the enemy before them. In this charge I regret that Colonel R. Matheson, Major George F. Lemon, *and Second Lieutenant Collins, of the Thirty-second New York, were severely wounded, and Second Lieutenant Wright killed; also, in the Eighteenth New York, Captain William Horsfall killed and Lieutenants Daley and Ellis wounded severely.—I take great pleasure in again noticing the gallantry and efficiency of Colonel R. Matheson, Thirty-second New York Volunteers, and who has been repeatedly recommended for promotion; also that of* Major George F. Lemon, *Thirty-second New York Volunteers.*[314]*

Caught up in the dramatic charge against Confederate forces at the base of Crampton's Gap and then the pursuit over South Mountain, the 32nd New York sustained significant casualties. Losses were reported as one officer and ten enlisted men killed, three officers and thirty-seven enlisted men wounded and zero missing, for a total of fifty-one.[315]

An older enlistment, George Lemon was forty-five years old when he mustered into the field and staff of the 32nd New York Infantry as major of the regiment. He enlisted for two years, his date of commission being May 31, 1861. George's service records show him as "present" starting in May 1861 through the September/October 1861 period, when his status was "not stated." George was shown as "present" once again starting in March/April 1862. According to his records, he remained "present" until September 14, 1862.[316]

On that date, during the fighting at Crampton's Gap, Major Lemon was severely wounded in the left thigh. He was removed to a hospital in Burkittsville and treated. Initially his prognosis was good, with recovery thought to be certain. On October 23, 1862, Major Lemon was even promoted to lieutenant colonel of the 32nd New York. In early November, however, George Lemon began to bleed. Fearing that the femoral artery was at fault, pressure was applied to the leg for more than a day. When this did not stop the bleeding, it was decided that the artery needed to be secured

Left: Major George Frank Lemon, 32nd New York Infantry. *Right*: Back of Lemon's image.

and the leg was removed using the flap method on November 9. Sadly, George Lemon did not recover and passed away on November 10, 1862, at Burkittsville, Maryland. Upon examination of the limb, it was discovered that the bullet that wounded him did indeed brush the artery, which had an ulcer a third of an inch long.[317] There is a note in his service records that his son came and collected his effects.

ORIGINALLY, THE REVERSE OF Major George Lemon's CDV was blank, with no information regarding the photographer or the major. A previous collector, however, identified Major Lemon and added pertinent information from his records. The front of the image is a bust view of the major, and although it is limited, we can still get quite a bit of information from it.

Being part of the regimental command meant that Major George Lemon wore a double-breasted dark-blue frock coat. As can be seen, this coat had a double row of seven buttons, which helped establish rank.[318] Six of the buttons are visible and appear to be New York State buttons, with their prominent ring design. On each of the major's shoulder are his shoulder boards. Though washed out in this image, they would have a gold oak leaf at each end of the board.[319]

Another intricacy of this image is the line that runs from the fourth button on his right side up to the second button on his left. The line appears to slip in behind the button on the right side and is more than likely a watch chain of some type. Finally, Major Lemon has a new paper collar for the photograph and has neatly trimmed and combed his beard and hair.

THE FIGHTING AT CRAMPTON'S Gap came to a close around 7:00 p.m. with darkness covering the field. The Union VI Corps controlled the gap, allowing the lead elements of the corps to press on into Pleasant Valley. After watching Confederate forces in Pleasant Valley, the men of the VI Corps were ordered to rejoin the Army of the Potomac on the night of September 16.[320] The following day they were again in action, this time at the Battle of Antietam. Their actions during America's single bloodiest day were limited, but those who had fought at Crampton's Gap were proud of their service during the Maryland Campaign.

Of the soldiers who fought at Crampton's Gap, three—Sergeant Aikens, First Lieutenant Edgerton and Second Lieutenant Rich—lived to the twentieth century. Major Lemon was mortally wounded at Crampton's Gap, while Sergeant Aikens, Sergeant Major Campbell and Second Lieutenant Rich were all wounded on other fields. Only First Lieutenant Edgerton and Private Wintermute returned from the war physically unscathed.

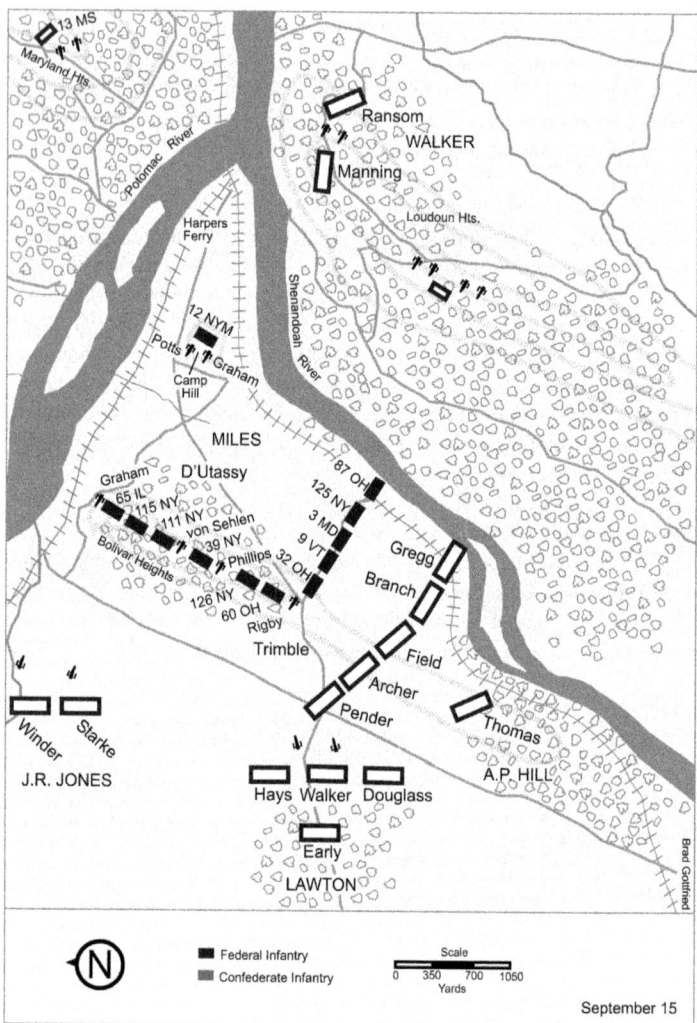

Capture of Harpers Ferry, September 15, 3:00 a.m.–7:00 a.m. *Map provided by Dr. Bradley Gottfried.*

Chapter 5

HARPERS FERRY

On September 12, 1862, Confederate forces began closing in on the Union garrison at Harpers Ferry. The Confederates were coming from three directions: Major General Thomas "Stonewall" Jackson's forces from the north and west, Major General Lafayette McLaws from the east and north and Brigadier General John Walker from the south. The fighting on the Maryland side of the Potomac, known as Maryland Heights, began on September 13. Two Confederate brigades moved toward the Union positions on the high ground overlooking the Potomac, forcing the Federals to retreat late that day. General Jackson's men approached the Union positions on Bolivar Heights on September 13, while General Walker's men were across the Shenandoah River on Loudoun Heights in Virginia. All began moving artillery into position to bombard the garrison. By late morning, Union forces in Harpers Ferry were surrounded. The next day, Jackson commenced a bombardment from three directions, paralyzing the garrison. On September 15, 1862, following the flanking of the Federal line on Bolivar Heights, Jackson initiated another bombardment, and soon the Union garrison surrendered.

The map presents the locations of the defenders of Harpers Ferry on the morning of September 15, at the time of the surrender. The Union forces are deployed in an "L" formation, with one leg along Bolivar Heights and the other leg attempting to anchor itself on the Shenandoah River. Closest to the Shenandoah was the 87th Ohio Infantry of Colonel William Ward's Brigade, along with the 125th New York Infantry, which was to the right of the 87th Ohio. The next unit represented is the 9th Vermont Infantry, part of Colonel William Trimble's Brigade. They were between the 32nd Ohio and the 3rd Maryland Potomac Home Brigade. On Bolivar Heights were additional units, including the 126th New York, which was also a part of Trimble's Brigade. To its right was the 111th New York Infantry from Colonel Fredrick D'Utassy's Brigade. The final unit represented here is the 115th New York Infantry, also from Colonel D'Utassy's Brigade. Most of these units had been in service less than three weeks or only a few months. The Battle of Harpers Ferry was their introduction to the war.

87TH OHIO INFANTRY

The 87th Ohio Infantry was organized at Camp Chase on June 10, 1862, to serve for three months. The regiment was first sent to Baltimore, Maryland, and after several weeks of training was ordered to Harpers Ferry, Virginia, to guard the city and surrounding area. It was there that the 87th Ohio was swept up with the capture of the Union garrison during the Battle of Harpers Ferry in September 1862. Instead of being marched south, the men were released on parole and sent to Camp Parole near Annapolis, Maryland. With its term of service coming to a close, the regiment was released from parole and sent home. The 87th Ohio Infantry was mustered out October 1–4, 1862, by reason of expiration of term of service.[321]

On September 14, the 87th Ohio was deployed in the lower part of the town of Harpers Ferry guarding the bridges. The regiment then moved to the left end of the Union line to fill the gap between Bolivar Heights and the Shenandoah River.[322] By the morning of September 15, the 87th Ohio was facing Confederate Major General Ambrose Powell Hill's infantry and artillery. The Ohio men were also subject to Confederate artillery fire from Loudoun Heights, across the Shenandoah River. With Harpers Ferry surrounded and the Confederates now poised on the flank of the Federal defenders, the Union position was no longer tenable. With the surrender of the Harpers Ferry garrison, the 87th Ohio reported 38 officers and 976 enlisted men captured, 1 enlisted killed and none wounded.[323]

The commander of the 87th Ohio at Harpers Ferry was Henry Banning, a man already a veteran of Civil War service. Banning began his service to the country as a captain in Company B of the 4th Ohio Infantry. He was commissioned on April 20, 1861, when his regiment was called up for three months of service. The 4th Ohio, however, was reformed as a three-year regiment, and Henry was mustered into it on June 1, 1861, as a captain, still in Company B. Just twenty-seven years old, Henry mustered out of the 4th Ohio on June 25, 1862, to accept the colonelcy and command of the newly formed 87th Ohio Infantry, another three-month unit. Following the debacle at Harpers Ferry, Colonel Banning was discharged at the end of the three months on October 4, 1862. Henry's service was not over yet, however, for on January 1, 1863, he became the lieutenant colonel of the 125th Ohio Infantry. He served to April 6, 1863, when he transferred to the 121st Ohio still as lieutenant colonel. On November 11, 1863, Henry was promoted to full colonel. However, something happened, for on September 4, 1864, this promotion was revoked. Perhaps due to this, Colonel Banning resigned on January 21, 1865. Still, he was not through with his service, for on March 20, 1865, he mustered into the 195th Ohio as colonel of the regiment. After garrison duty in the south, Henry finally completed his service on December 18, 1865. Henry Banning was given a brevet promotion to first brigadier and later major general to date from March 13, 1865, for meritorious services during the war. After the war, Henry was a lawyer and served in the Ohio House of Representatives for a year before being elected to Congress for three terms from 1873 to 1879. He died unexpectedly on December 10, 1881, in Cincinnati, Ohio. He was forty-five at the time of his death, having been born on November 10, 1836, in Banning's Mills, Knox County, Ohio. Henry Banning is buried at Spring Grove Cemetery, Garden LN, Section 80, Lot 43, Space 1.[324]

THE IMAGE OF HENRY Banning is curious, not only because of his appearance but also due to where it was taken. According to the advertisement on the back of the CDV, this image was taken by E.W. Beckwith of Alexandria, Virginia. No other information, such as a tax stamp or writing, has been provided, although a more recent collector marked the back with Banning's name and his rank in this photo, a brigadier general. Once an officer is brevetted above the rank of lieutenant colonel, he may wear the uniform of the brevet rank if he so chooses.[325] In the case of Henry Banning, his rank was a colonel, but due to his brevets he was welcome to wear the uniform of a brigadier or even major general.

Henry Banning's brevet promotions came after the Atlanta Campaign and the Battle of Nashville. Both of these events occurred in late 1864. At the end of the war, Banning was commanding the 195th Ohio Infantry

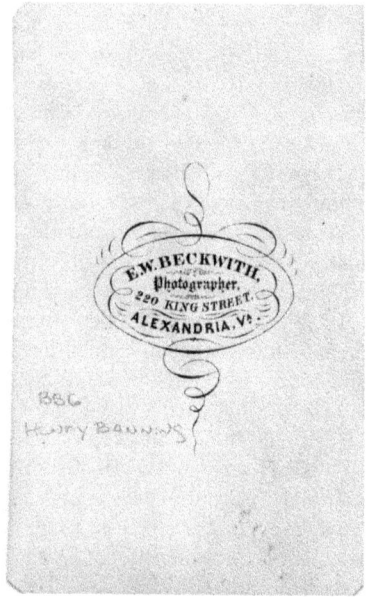

Left: Colonel Henry Banning, 87th Ohio Infantry. *Right*: Back of Banning's image.

and based out of Alexandria, Virginia.[326] This was likely when he had this image taken. However, that would have been in 1865, and the luxury tax on CDVs was not repealed until August 1866,[327] so where is the stamp for this image? There is no evidence of it being removed. While it is possible that the photographer may have waived the tax for some reason, it is also possible that this was actually taken several years after the war, when Banning was serving in Congress. Alexandria is just across the Potomac River from Washington. Perhaps he used some props provided by the photographer to rebuild his general's uniform for the image.

The Beckwith Studio provided a small table with decorative cloth, along with a large book, perhaps a Bible, for both decoration and to rest against. The tablecloth, as well as Henry Banning's legs, are hiding the base of the brace he is using to help keep his head steady. A foot of that brace can be seen just behind his right shoe. Henry's shoes are private purchase and as such are of higher quality than the enlisted man's shoe. In this case, the smooth side of the leather is out, making for any easier polish and shine.

Harpers Ferry

Henry Banning is wearing either very dark-blue or black pants. One of his biographies commented on the velveteen pants, which "gave him anything but a military appearance"[328] while in the field. Whether the image was taken at the end of the war or several years later, it is interesting to note that these are dark pants, as opposed to sky blue, and that they are without the eighth-of-an-inch light-blue piping down the seam.[329]

The double-breasted frock coat worn here has a long skirt, nearly reaching the knees, and is an excellent example of the officer's frock. The four parallel sets of two buttons distinguish the frock immediately as that of a brigadier general's, as do the single-star shoulder boards,[330] the left one being almost fully visible. The coat has voluminous sleeves, which had become popular with the officer's frock, as opposed to the close-fitting enlisted frock. It also has the velvet cuffs and collar and the three cuff buttons prominent on an officer's frock.[331] Finally, a soft, unadorned slouch hat sits atop Henry Banning's head, and he also neatly trimmed his beard and combed his hair for the image.

125ᵀᴴ NEW YORK INFANTRY

Recruited in Rensselaer County, the 125th New York Infantry was mustered into service August 27–29, 1862, for three years. Two days later, the regiment left for Harpers Ferry, where it was captured on September 15, due to the surrender of that post. Paroled by Confederate forces, the 125th New York was ordered to Camp Douglas, Chicago, Illinois, to wait out the war until notified that its members had been exchanged for Confederate prisoners of war. The regiment was declared exchanged and returned to Virginia in December. The 125th New York spent several months in the defenses of Washington before being assigned to the Army of the Potomac, with which it stayed for the rest of its service. Having fought through the Gettysburg Campaign, at Bristoe Station and Mine Run, the Overland Campaign, the Siege of Petersburg and the Appomattox Campaign, the 125th New York Infantry mustered out near Alexandria, Virginia, on June 5, 1865, having earned the title as a fighting regiment.[332]

Present during the Battle of Harpers Ferry, Colonel George L. Willard, the commander of the 125th New York, wrote of the actions of the regiment:

> *About 1 o'clock p. m., on the 14th September, the enemy, who had succeeded in establishing a battery of rifled guns on Loudoun Heights, opened with*

shot and shell upon my regiment, which, having just returned from picket duty, were engaged in preparing some food. The fire was rapid, and all the troops on the plateau made a speedy and somewhat disorderly retreat. My regiment, in spite of my efforts, and subjected for the first time to a hot fire, retreated in a good deal of disorder toward the ravine running south from the battery on Bolivar Heights. At this point I succeeded in rallying them, and reformed the regiment on the east side, where it remained until ordered to cross to the west. Here two companies (Captains Cornell and Wood) were detached, by order of Brigadier-General White, to support two guns which had been ordered to advance. With the remaining eight companies I was directed, by the same officer, to occupy the ravine on the road leading to the Shenandoah…

On my right was the Third Maryland and Ninth Vermont Regiments. During the night I called upon the commanding officer of the Third Maryland, Lieutenant-Colonel Downey, and with him on Colonel Stannard, of Ninth Vermont, and, upon consultation, a request was sent to Colonel Trimble, Sixtieth Ohio, commanding brigade, to grant us an interview, in the hope that some change might be made in the disposition of the troops, as we had become aware that the enemy had placed batteries on the opposite side of the Shenandoah, which it was believed would make our line of defense untenable…

At daylight on the 15th September the enemy opened from the batteries which he had placed in position during the night, and was replied to by the two guns which had been placed in rear of the right wing of my regiment. The fire was very severe, and continued until about 8 o'clock a.m., when, to my astonishment, I saw a white flag raised from the battery on Bolivar Heights.

The firing from the enemy's batteries did not immediately stop, and I remained with my regiment in position until there was not to my knowledge any guns or troops on my right, all having retired and the firing ceased. Forty-five minutes after the raising of the white flag I ordered the regiment to retire, which was done in good order, although subjected to an artillery fire from Loudoun Heights, which opened on my regiment and killed 2 of my men. I ordered the regimental colors to be torn from the staff and destroyed, to prevent them from falling into the hands of the enemy.[333]

Captured with the rest of the Harpers Ferry garrison, the 125th New York reported 38 officers and 881 enlisted men captured or missing, as well as 2 men killed and 1 man wounded.[334]

Among the captured was Captain Samuel Armstrong of Company D, 125th New York Infantry. He was commissioned on September 10, 1862, at Troy, New York. He gave his age as twenty-three when he signed up for three years of service. His service records show him as "present" from August 27 to October 31, 1862. During this period, Samuel was taken prisoner at Harpers Ferry on September 15, 1862. Captain Armstrong wrote about his experience at Harpers Ferry: "I tell you, it is dreadful to be a mark of artillery, Bad enough for any but especially for raw troops; it demoralizes them—it rouses one's courage to be able to fight in return, but to sit still and calmly be cut in two is too much to ask."[335]

Once paroled, Samuel Armstrong was "present" through the period the 125th New York spent at Camp Douglas, Chicago, and was with the regiment when it returned to the east. He was "absent" on July 28, 1863, on detached duty at Rikers Island, which was at the time used as a training camp for new regiments and the rendezvous for draftees. Armstrong remained in New York until November 1, 1863. On that date, Samuel was promoted to major; twelve days later, he was transferred as a lieutenant colonel to the 9th United States Colored Troops. One year later, on November 3, 1864, Samuel was promoted to the colonelcy of the 8th USCT and commanded the regiment until after the war. Samuel's service ended when he mustered out on November 10, 1865. He had received a brevet promotion to brigadier general as of March 13, 1865, for meritorious services.[336]

Inspired by his early life in Hawaii, where he was born on January 30, 1839, to his missionary parents, as well as from his time with the United States Colored Troops, Samuel Armstrong joined the Freedmen's Bureau after the Civil War and established the Hampton Normal and Agricultural Institute, now known as Hampton University, in Hampton, Virginia, in 1868. He remained with the Institute until his death on May 11, 1893, in Hampton, Virginia. Today, he is buried at the Hampton University Cemetery and honored with a statue on the university grounds.[337]

THE IMAGE OF SAMUEL Armstrong was taken by Brady's National Portrait Gallery. Mathew Brady had galleries in both New York and Washington, which is reflected on the photographer's advertisement on the back of the image. While Samuel Armstrong did spend considerable time in New York in 1863, it is also possible this was taken after the 125th New York's return to the east when it was stationed in Washington. This bust shot shows a dark-blue double-breasted frock, with the buttons, only one of

Left: Captain Samuel Armstrong, 125th New York Infantry. *Right*: Back of Armstrong's image.

which is visible, aligned on the outer edge of the chest. Other images of Samuel Armstrong in the same or a very similar frock show that there are seven buttons in two angled rows that frame the chest. These parallel rows of seven represent an officer in the command staff of a regiment.[338] The buttons would not have been general service Federal eagles, but instead would have been officer's buttons with the infantry "I" on the shield the eagle is holding.[339]

Armstrong signed the back of the image with his initials and apparently listed his address, "34 Wall St, NY," so this was probably used as a calling card. A previous collector also wrote down some biographical information about Armstrong. To finish off the image, Samuel Armstrong has on a clean paper collar or freshly starched white shirt, though no cravat. He is also clean shaven but has taken the time to comb his hair for posterity.

9ᵀᴴ Vermont Infantry

On May 21, 1862, Vermont governor Frederick Holbrook was ordered by the War Department to reopen recruiting in the state and raise another regiment of infantry. By recruiting in twelve different counties, the quota for what became the 9th Vermont Infantry was reached in a very short amount of time. In less than two months, on July 9, the 920 officers and men of the 9th Vermont Infantry were assembled and mustered into United States service.[340]

By July 15, the regiment was off by train to Washington, where it was attached to the division of Brigadier General Samuel Sturgis on July 19. Five days later, the 9th Vermont was on its way to the Shenandoah Valley. In early August, the regiment was attached to the brigade of Brigadier General Julius White and put to work building fortifications near Winchester, Virginia. With the advance of Confederate forces in early September, White was ordered to fall back to Martinsburg and eventually Harpers Ferry, where the 9th Vermont was detached and placed in the brigade of Colonel William Trimble.[341]

Skirmishing began on Maryland Heights, above Harpers Ferry, on September 13. By that afternoon, Confederate forces had taken the heights, and Confederate activity was observed to the south on Loudoun Heights. During the afternoon of September 14, Confederate batteries opened from Loudoun Heights. Captain Edward Ripley, commanding Company B, 9th Vermont Infantry at the time, wrote of this unexpected bombardment: "Major [Edwin S.] Stowell and I lay and watched them with our glasses uneasily, when suddenly, in the center of White's Brigade, lying at our feet. There was a crash, then another, and another and columns of dirt and smoke leaped up as though a dozen vigorous volcanoes had broken forth, Stowell caught the situation quicker than I, and exclaimed, 'Good God! It's their guns!'" Ripley continued: "All at once one dropped in my Company's street, which let all the humor out of it. Then in a cool and quiet way the Companies fell into line and marched deliberately up over the crest of the hill and lay down, where the shells skipped over our heads into the valley beyond. For a space of time we did the best we could by moving over from one slope to another. Whichever slope we were on, we wished it were the other."[342]

The bombardment, as well as the subsequent movements of Confederate troops under the command of Major General A.P. Hill on the night of September 14–15, led to the capture of the garrison. At Harpers Ferry, the 9th Vermont reported 30 officers and 714 enlisted men captured or missing, none killed and 3 enlisted men wounded.[343]

The next four months were spent at Camp Douglas, Chicago, as paroled prisoners. The 9th Vermont was exchanged on January 10, 1863, and remained at Camp Douglas as guards of the Confederate prisoners captured at the Battles of Murfreesboro and Arkansas Post. This thankless duty continued until about April 1, 1863. After this, the 9th Vermont was transferred east by detachments, escorting Confederate POWs to their exchange. Once reassembled, the Vermonters became part of the garrison of Suffolk, Virginia. At Suffolk, the 9th Vermont found itself besieged again, this time by the forces of Confederate Major General James Longstreet. For just over three weeks, fighting and skirmishing were nearly constant along the lines, but the siege failed. The 9th Vermont was then attached to the little-known and ill-fated attempt to take Richmond in the spring of 1863, although it was not directly involved in the fighting. The 9th Vermont spent the rest of 1863 and most of 1864 in and around first Yorktown, Virginia, then New Berne and Moorehead City, North Carolina. Numerous skirmishes were fought before the 9th Vermont was transferred to the Petersburg front as part of the Army of the James on September 15, 1864, the two-year anniversary of its capture at Harpers Ferry. Taking part in the late 1864 engagements around Petersburg and Richmond, the 9th Vermont was stationed outside Richmond's lines when the collapse of the Confederate defense occurred. Advancing on April 3, the regiment entered Richmond and remained there as its provost guard for the next two weeks. Finally, on June 13, 1865, the original members of the 9th Vermont Infantry were mustered out of service. Nearly four hundred recruits remained in the regiment until December before also being mustered out.[344]

Among those who had helped raise and lead the 9th Vermont Infantry was Charles Jarvis, born in Weathersfield, Vermont, on August 21, 1821.[345] A farmer before the war, Charles mustered into Company D, which he had raised, on July 9, 1862, as the company captain. Swept up with the rest of the regiment at Harpers Ferry, he became a prisoner of war on September 15, 1862. Captain Jarvis was sent to Camp Douglas near Chicago, Illinois, and was not back in the field until March 1863. On May 24, 1863, Charles was promoted to major of the regiment. Two months later, on July 24, Major Jarvis was sent to Vermont for recruiting duty. He returned to the regiment on September 25, 1863. The final event noted in Charles's service records was that he was killed in a skirmish on December 1, 1863, at Cedar Point, North Carolina. The 9th Vermont assistant surgeon W.S. Vincent's account states that the wound was caused by "a conical ball from a Colt Navy revolver."[346] Charles is buried at Bow Cemetery, Weathersfield, Vermont.

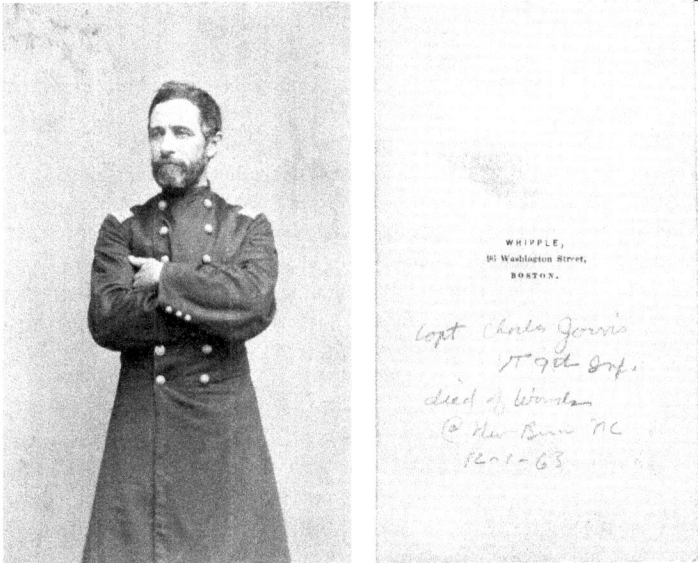

Left: Captain Charles Jarvis, 9th Vermont Infantry. *Right*: Back of Jarvis's image.

THE IMAGE OF MAJOR Charles Jarvis, taken at the Whipple Gallery in Boston, Massachusetts, was likely done while on his recruiting detail in the summer of 1863. Although the image was originally unsigned, a more recent collector wrote Jarvis's name, his regiment and his date of death on the back of the CDV. The image itself is a very basic standing view with no background decoration or anything to lean against. Thus, Major Jarvis chose to stand, arms folded.

The major's dark-blue frock coat is the commanding element in this image. The skirting, voluminous sleeves, three cuff buttons and short collar give the coat away as an officer's frock. The double row of seven eagle buttons is prominent, five of each row being visible, and indicates that this officer is part of the command staff of his regiment. In this case, Major Jarvis's shoulder boards are very apparent, and the gold oak leaf of a major's rank within the board can just barely be made out on his right shoulder.[347] Wearing no apparent cravat, Major Charles Jarvis has the trimmed beard and short hair popular with men in the field, as well as a determined look on his face.

126TH NEW YORK INFANTRY

Part of the summer 1862 recruiting campaign for "Three Hundred Thousand More," the 126th New York Infantry was recruited in the counties of Ontario, Seneca and Yates. The regiment was organized at Camp Swift, Geneva, and mustered into United States service for three years on August 22, 1862. Four days later, the 126th New York was ordered south, reaching Baltimore on August 27. From there, the New Yorkers were sent to guard Harpers Ferry, arriving on August 28.[348] During the Battle of Harpers Ferry, just over two weeks later, the 126th New York sustained significant casualties attempting to hold Maryland Heights above Harpers Ferry and afterward Bolivar Heights. Being part of the surrendered garrison, the 126th New York was paroled and sent to Camp Douglas, Chicago, where it remained under guard until December 1862. Once exchanged, the regiment was transported back east and was part of the Washington defenses until June 1863, when it was transferred to the II Corps. The 126th New York remained with the II Corps for the rest of the war, taking part in the many campaigns of the Army of the Potomac. By the end of 1864, the hard service of the 126th New York had forced the regiment to be consolidated into a battalion of five companies, A through E.

The 126th New York was finally mustered out in Washington on June 3, 1865. The total enrollment of the regiment during service was 1,036, while the total of killed and wounded in the regiment amounted to 535.[349]

During the fighting above Harpers Ferry on Maryland Heights, the 126th New York was in a precarious position. One history of the regiment noted:

> *The men of the 126th began firing at a still unseen foe, concealed by the haze and trees. The firing increased as the smoke created by the discharge of the black powder rifles began to cloud their vision even more. Finally, the order to fall back was given as the position became untenable. Colonel* [Eliakim] *Sherrill began forming the men of the 126th behind cover. He soon had reestablished his ranks and the men began firing to their front in an effort to prevent the rebels from advancing on their position. Sherrill was warned about exposing himself, when "a ball ripped through both cheeks, knocking out teeth and mangling his tongue." This forced his temporary retirement. "With their commander shot and their position being outflanked, the men of the 126th were accused of initiating a stampede that carried the surrounding units along with them." The 126th claimed that it received an order to withdraw by Colonel* [Thomas H.]

Ford. Regardless it was a confused situation and resulted in the Union forces leaving Maryland Heights.[350]

Between the fighting on the Maryland Heights and the later defense of Bolivar Heights, the 126th New York reported at the surrender of the garrison, 30 officers and 946 enlisted men captured or missing, as well as 1 officer and 12 enlisted men killed and 4 officers and 38 enlisted men wounded.[351]

Among the captured was Fayette Green, who had mustered in on August 22, 1862, into Company E of the 126th New York Infantry for three years of service. At the time, Fayette was a twenty-one-year old farmer, described in his service records as five feet, nine inches tall, with fair complexion, hazel eyes and light hair. He stated he was born in Rushville, New York. Fayette was mustered in as first sergeant of Company E and was captured on September 15, 1862, as part of the Harpers Ferry garrison. Something must have happened during his time at Camp Douglas, as Fayette Green was reduced to the ranks on October 19, 1862. Returned to the Eastern Theater in December 1862 with the rest of the 126th New York, now Private Green was "present" until June 1864. During that period, on January 1, 1863, he was promoted to fifth sergeant; on March 1, while serving as a clerk at Brigade Headquarters, he was promoted again, to third sergeant. Fayette's final promotion, to second lieutenant, took place on August 3, 1863. The following spring, on June 3, 1864, Lieutenant Green was Wounded in Action at Cold Harbor. Although no description of the wound has been found, it appears to have put him out of action. That August, Fayette Green's pay was reduced by $5.28 for transportation furnished by the government, and he was likely traveling to a hospital, as his records show that on June 11, 1864, he was sent to Patterson Park USA General Hospital in Baltimore, Maryland. On Christmas Day 1864, Lieutenant Green was mustered out of the service as a supernumerary due to the consolidation of the regiment. He had last been paid on February 29, 1864, and owed the government $13.26 for his clothing allowance. However, he was still due $75.00 from his enlistment bounty.[352] Fayette filed for a pension on August 30, 1883,[353] and passed away six years later on December 23, 1889. He is buried at Arlington National Cemetery and can be found in Section 13, headstone no. 13714.[354]

The image of Fayette Green was taken by photographer Opperman at Wolff's Gallery in Alexandria, Virginia. Green signed the back of the image, under the stylized gallery advertisement, "B F Green 126th NY," indicating

Left: Private Fayette Green, 126th New York Infantry. *Right*: Back of Green's image.

this CDV was likely used as a calling card. There is no record as to what the "B" stands for, as all of Green's records and the regimental roster list him as Fayette Green. The studio provided a draped column to lean against, as well as a stand to brace his head for this image. The studio has a thin carpet and may have a blank background set up behind Green; there appears to be a gap between the wall behind him and the floor. The image itself was probably taken while the 126th New York was stationed in the defenses of Washington. This defensive ring included Alexandria. As Green is shown as a private in this photograph, it is safe to assume this was taken either in very late 1862 or early 1863, after the 126th New York had returned from parole and Green had been reduced to the rank of private.

Standing in a relaxed pose, Fayette Green is wearing the issued government shoe, or Jefferson bootee.[355] In this case, the shoes may be a recent issue, as they are very dark and polished. His trousers are the sky blue kersey wool of the volunteers, above which a dark-blue vest can be seen. While the vest allowed Green to have his coat fully open, he has chosen to keep the top button of his nine-button frock buttoned. Although only seven of the frock's eagle buttons are visible, there are eight buttonholes that can be seen—the ninth is at the connecting point of the frock and the skirting. The frock coat's two small eagle cuff buttons are plainly visible on his left sleeve, while one can be seen on the right. This particular frock coat also has the light-blue piping on the cuffs and collar indicating the infantry branch of the service.[356] The collar piping has even been lightly colored blue on the image. Green is a private in this photograph and thus has no indication of rank on either his frock or trousers.

Fayette Green has a neatly trimmed beard and combed his hair for this image. On his head is his forage cap. The forage cap design varied greatly from contractor to contractor. In this case, the cap has a large, stiff, squared bill and is likely a variation on the Model 1858 forage cap.[357] One of the two small eagle buttons used to secure the chin strap can be seen on the right side of Green's head.

111ᵀᴴ NEW YORK INFANTRY

The 111th New York Infantry was organized at Auburn from companies recruited in Cayuga and Wayne Counties and was mustered into the United States service on August 20, 1862. The regiment left Auburn the following day for Harpers Ferry. There, after less than a month's service, the 111th New York was captured with the rest of the garrison on September 15, 1862. The men were paroled and sent to Camp Douglas, Chicago, where they remained until December. Shipped back east, the 111th New York went into winter quarters at Centerville, Virginia. During the winter of 1863, the regiment was assigned to the defenses of Washington with the XXII Corps. Reassigned to the II Corps in June 1863, the regiment remained with this corps for the rest of the war and was mustered out near Alexandria, Virginia, on June 3, 1865.[358]

As stated in General Julius White's report, the 111th New York was stationed on Bolivar Heights during the Battle of Harpers Ferry: "The right of Bolivar Heights was held by the brigade under command of Colonel D'Utassy, of the Thirty-ninth New York, consisting of the Thirty-ninth, One hundred and eleventh, and One hundred and fifteenth New York, the Sixty-fifth Illinois, and Captains Phillips and Von Sehlen's batteries. A slight earth-work was constructed upon the right, to protect the men of the batteries."[359]

Prior to the surrender of the garrison, during the struggle for the Maryland Heights, the 111th New York reported losses of 5 enlisted men killed and 6 men wounded. On September 15, 1862, 36 officers and 934 enlisted men of the 111th New York surrendered with the rest of the Harpers Ferry garrison.[360]

Captured with the 111th New York was Howard Servis, who enlisted as a private in Company B on August 20, 1862. As noted in the company descriptive book, he was twenty-two years old and five feet, eight and a half inches tall, with black hair, hazel eyes and a dark complexion. He was born in New York and worked as a farmer before enlisting. Howard was listed as "present" from his muster to February 11, 1863. During this period, he was promoted to corporal and then sergeant, although the dates of these promotions have not been provided. On February 11, 1863, Servis was detached from the regiment and sent to New York to arrest deserters. He remained on detached duty until April 11, 1863. Howard was next detached to Arlington, Virginia, on June 4, 1863, as acting quartermaster. In between these dates, Howard was promoted to second lieutenant as of April 13, 1863. During May/June of that year, Howard became sick and was absent. When he returned to duty is not clear, but his trouble with sickness had just begun. Howard was reported sick again on July 26, 1864, but was present during September/October 1864. On October 16, 1864, Howard mustered as the first lieutenant of Company G, although he may have been acting as a first lieutenant since February 2, 1864. For November/December, Howard was present and due an additional ten dollars per month for April/May/June/October for having been acting regimental quartermaster. In February 1865, Lieutenant Servis was "sick in quarters." He was due an additional ten dollars as commander of the company in February. On March 8, 1865, Howard was sent to the hospital at City Point, sick. He was noted in the surgeon's reports as having diarrhea. This is likely what led to his discharge from service on May 15, 1865.[361]

Howard Servis had last been paid on December 31, 1864. He was appointed a captain on May 15, 1865, but never assumed the rank.[362] According to Howard's pension index card, he filed for a pension on August 16, 1889. Howard died on February 13, 1921, in Ellington, New York.[363] He is buried in his family plot at Fort Hill Cemetery, Auburn, New York, Ridgeland section, Lot 39, Grave 3.[364]

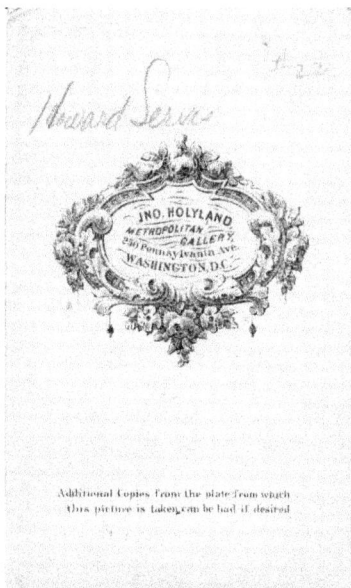

Left: Private Howard Servis, 111th New York Infantry. *Right*: Back of Servis's image.

ACCORDING TO THE ADVERTISEMENT on the back of this image, Lieutenant Howard Servis had this taken by Jonathan Holyland of the Metropolitan Gallery in Washington. As Servis signed the back of this CDV as well as the front with his rank and regiment, it is probable that he used this image as a calling card. The image was likely taken in the summer of 1863. Howard had been promoted to second lieutenant by that point, and he was on detached duty in Arlington, Virginia, just across the Potomac River from the capital. With his proximity to Washington and his new rank as an officer, there was no better time to have an image done.

The Metropolitan Gallery utilized several decorations of the period for this image, such as the pedestal and column. As with most other standing images of the day, a brace was provided to help steady Howard Servis's head for the photograph. The foot of the brace can be seen behind Howard's right shoe. The shoes themselves have quite a shine and may be a new purchase. Lieutenant Servis is wearing his sky blue officer trousers and has the eighth-of-an-inch dark-blue piping running up the seam to help designate his rank.[365] The rank indicator on his trousers is very helpful because the rest of Servis's uniform is obscured by his greatcoat. A private purchase, this civilian coat may even be a prop provided by the gallery. The greatcoat is black or very dark blue, with a black silk braid to bind the edges. Four cloth buttons are visible on this coat, with possibly a fifth just under the collar. Worn open, the vest underneath can be seen; six of its nine buttons are visible, although most of the buttons are undone, probably for ventilation. Some sort of chain, likely for a watch, can also be seen between the first and second buttons from the bottom of the vest.

Sitting beside Howard Servis is his kepi. It appears to be a standard Model 1858 with a stiff leather visor. What is interesting about this kepi is the branch insignia. Appropriate for an infantry officer, the hunter's horn is prominent. However, this particular horn looks more like a brass decoration, as opposed to the embroidered patch of an officer.[366] This could mean that the bugle is actually stamped brass imitating embroidery,[367] or it could be a prop used in place of an officer's kepi Servis has yet to get. Howard is also sporting a neatly trimmed goatee and mustache for this image and combed his dark hair.

115TH NEW YORK INFANTRY

The 115th New York, referred to as the "Iron Hearts" in its regimental history for its stand at the Battle of Olustee, was recruited during July and August 1862 in the counties of Fulton, Hamilton, Montgomery and Saratoga. The regiment was organized at Camp Mohawk in Fonda, New York, the home of its original colonel, Simeon Sammons.[368] The 115th New York was mustered into the United States service on August 26, 1862, for three years. Four days later, the regiment left the state and proceeded to Sandy Hook, Maryland, located one mile down the Potomac River from Harpers Ferry. The 115th New York received its arms and accoutrements while at Sandy Hook. Unfortunately, the New Yorkers were forced to surrender two weeks later with the capitulation of the Harpers Ferry garrison. Along with most of the garrison, the 115th New York was paroled and sent to Camp Douglas, Chicago, to await exchange. This occurred on November 20, and the 115th New York returned to the east. From there it was sent to Hilton Head and Beaufort, South Carolina, before being transferred to Florida. The 115th New York was later attached to the X Corps and the Army of the James, with which it fought through the Bermuda Hundred and Petersburg Campaigns. Finally, the regiment was transferred to the XXIV Corps and sent to North Carolina, where it was involved in the campaigns to close the Confederate port of Wilmington. The regiment was mustered out at Raleigh, North Carolina, on June 17, 1865. Out of a total enrollment of 1,196, the 115th New York lost 7 officers and 132 men to combat, as well as 191 men dead of disease and other causes, for a total of 330.[369]

The 115th New York was briefly involved with the skirmishing on Maryland Heights on September 13, 1862. After the heights were abandoned, the regiment was ordered back to Bolivar Heights, where it was subject to the Confederate bombardment on September 14. The regiment history describes the action as following:

> *At 4o'clock P.M., we received orders to fall in line of battle in the rear of Bolivar Heights, along the edge of a piece of woods.—shell after shell exploded around about us, above and among the marching column—a single line of battle formed of all the Union troops, the 115th holding the extreme right. The Union soldiers all lay flat on the ground to avoid the shells which the rebels were pouring in upon them. They would get a complete range of our line, and then concentrate the fire of all the batteries they had on a given point. In that way they made it too hot for any troops to stand; so we were obliged to change our line very frequently, to save the men from slaughter.*[370]

Though captured at Harpers Ferry, the 115th New York reported few actual injuries from the skirmishing and bombardment. The regiment listed 28 officers and 950 enlisted men captured or missing, none killed and only 1 officer and 10 enlisted men wounded.[371]

One of the new recruits captured at Harpers Ferry was Ezra W. Drake, who had mustered into Company F of the 115th New York Volunteers on August 14, 1862. He enlisted as a private for three years. His descriptive book page notes Ezra as being twenty-seven and five feet, eight and a half inches tall, with a light complexion, blue eyes and light hair; he was born in Greenfield, New York. One source lists his occupation at enlistment as a glass blower, but another says blacksmith. Private Drake was "present" from August 25 to October 31, 1862. A note in his records says that he was assigned as a hospital nurse on September 10. Ezra was shown as detailed to the hospital at Camp Vermont, Virginia, in November 1862. He was also described as a "hospital cook" as of September 8, 1862. He continued to be "present" though September/October 1863. In November/December 1863, Ezra was detached for daily duty with the regimental band. This was his assignment until September/October 1864, when he was listed as being a part of the "Brigade Band." On June 17, 1865, Ezra mustered out of the service at Raleigh, North Carolina. He had last been paid on December 31, 1864, and had drawn $33.14 against his clothing allowance as of August 31, 1864. Fortunately, he was still due $75.00 of his enlistment bounty.[372] Ezra died on January 9, 1892, and is buried at North Milton Cemetery, Saratoga County, New York. His widow filed for a survivor's pension on February 3, 1892.[373]

THIS IMAGE OF EZRA Drake is interesting, as the photographer's advertisement on the back says it was taken in Boston, Massachusetts, by J.W. Black. However, the 115th New York did not pass through Boston on its various travels during the war. Nor was Ezra Drake himself ordered to Boston or its vicinity. It is possible that Drake had this taken on his way home in 1865, but the image is lacking the luxury tax stamp for CDVs that were in use from August 1864 to August 1866.[374]

With a simple drapery for decoration, Ezra Drake stands with arms folded looking just over the shoulder of the photographer. He is wearing the light-blue kersey wool trousers of the volunteers and has a long, dark-blue frock coat. The frock has the usual defining features: the skirting; the piping at the collar and cuffs, in this case light-blue for the infantry; and the two cuff buttons. Both can be seen on Drake's right cuff, with one on his left. The frock would have had nine buttons running down the chest, although only five are visible in this image. The buttons themselves may be New York state seal buttons, as they appear to have the prominent ring design[375] as opposed to the large eagle buttons of most Federal coats. What is different about this frock is what it is potentially lacking. Ezra Drake started out as a hospital steward and cook in the 115th New York, but he was transferred to the regimental and later the Brigade Band. If he was with the band at the time of this image, he could have had a much more decorative frock. Musicians could have a worsted lace bib sewn onto their jacket front in a herring bone pattern. The color of the lacing was the branch color; in this case it would have been sky blue.[376]

Ezra Drake is wearing a high collared shirt under his frock, likely with a new paper collar. He also has on his forage cap. This particular cap appears to be a "McDowell," named after the commanding general at the First

Left: Private Ezra W. Drake, 115th New York Infantry. *Right*: Back of Drake's image.

Battle of Bull Run, Irvin McDowell. It is a variation of the Model 1858 forage cap with a short, curved leather visor.[377] Drake's forage cap has the usual leather adjusting band, as well as an infantry hunter's horn in brass on the crown. Finally, he has a magnificent mustache, which has been trimmed and possibly waxed, as well as the deep-set, almost haunted eyes of a man who has seen something of the horrors of war.

ALL SIX OF THESE men fought to defend Harpers Ferry and suffered the shame of the garrison's surrender at 8:00 a.m. on September 15, 1862. Following the surrender and their parole, all returned to duty. Two of these soldiers, Banning and Armstrong, were brevetted brigadier general for their service later in the war. Both of them passed away in the nineteenth century. Captain Jarvis paid the ultimate price of service and was killed in action on December 1, 1863. Sergeant Green was Wounded in Action in the Wilderness in June 1864 but recovered enough be mustered out later that year. Private Servis survived the greatest killer in the army, sickness, and lived into the twentieth century. The final member of the group, Private Drake, was not on the front lines, as he was assigned to the hospital and later the band. He passed away in 1892. These six men served their country through what became the largest surrender of United States forces prior to the fall of Bataan in 1942. They and their comrades were occasionally ridiculed for this, but they persevered and served out the rest of their enlistments with honor.

EPILOGUE

The fighting at South Mountain was unique for the American Civil War. Not only were the forces engaged confined to fairly limited areas of the mountain, the gaps, due to the nature of the terrain, but also the fighting did not end with the day. Specifically, the fighting at Turner's, Frosttown and Crampton's Gaps continued until after dark, with men directing their fire by the sounds and muzzle flashes of their opponents. When it was over, these men slumped down on the field of battle or nearby. Numerous soldiers wrote after the battle about bedding down among the dead and wounded following the fighting. For others, the day's work was not yet complete, as hospital stewards and stretcher bearers did their best to retrieve the wounded from the field. Brought to numerous hospitals set up below South Mountain, in the houses and farms along the National Road or in the dwellings of Burkittsville, the wounded were cared for by the surgeons, who did their best to save lives. In the end, the fighting at the four gaps in South Mountain cost approximately 2,346 men from the Union's I, VI and IX Corps.[378] Confederate records for South Mountain are incomplete, but most estimates have them as comparable with Union losses, putting total estimates casualties of the battle at just over 5,000 killed, wounded, missing or captured.

Where the fighting at the South Mountain gaps had been heavily contested, the situation was far different at Harpers Ferry. The early loss of the Maryland Heights above Harpers Ferry, along with completely ignoring the potential threat of Loudoun Heights, doomed the garrison. Confederate forces were able to close on Harpers Ferry from three directions, placing their artillery on the dominating terrain and hemming the garrison in. For the Union garrison, their only hope was the Army of the Potomac, but the Confederate presence at Crampton's Gap saw to that, slowing the VI Corps' advance. The only bright spot was a dash on the night of September 14, 1862, by the Union cavalry that allowed approximately 1,500 horse soldiers to escape Harpers Ferry. The next morning, by 8:00 a.m., 12,737 Union soldiers had become prisoners of war.[379] Included in this haul were seventy-three cannons, twelve to thirteen thousand small arms, nearly two hundred wagons and more than 1,000 freedmen, all of which was sent under guard to Winchester, Virginia.[380]

With the collapse of the Confederate defense of South Mountain and the fall of Harpers Ferry, all eyes turned west, toward Washington County, Maryland. Over the next two days, the fields and farms surrounding the small crossroads town of Sharpsburg, Maryland, saw the influx of thousands upon thousands of soldiers in blue and gray. Robert E. Lee had been beaten once, but with the return of Jackson's command, he was not yet ready to give up on his efforts on Northern soil. The bloodiest single day of the war was yet to come.

Often overshadowed by the much larger and bloodier Battle of Antietam, these early battles in Maryland Campaign set the stage for that climactic clash. Today, the battlefield landscapes discussed here are remarkably intact. It is possible to go to each of the South Mountain Gaps, three of which are now part of the Maryland State Park System, as well as Harpers Ferry, which is administered by the National Park Service as the Harpers Ferry National Historic Site. The State of Maryland, the National Park Service and the preservation partners of both endeavor to preserve and protect these natural and historic landscapes for future generations. All the while, they hope that visitors will utilize these landscapes for their own education and recreation. We encourage you to visit these sites, walk the trails and climb the heights scaled more than 155 years by thousands of men in Union blue and Confederate gray.

Notes

Introduction

1. Darrah, *Cartes de Visite*, 87.
2. Antietam on the Web, "Lee's Letter to President Davis on Moving into Maryland."
3. Radcliffe, *Governor Thomas H. Hicks of Maryland*, 73–74.
4. Foreman, *World on Fire*, 295.
5. U.S. War Department, Moody, Cowles, Ainsworth et al., *War of the Rebellion: A Compilation of the Official Records of the Union and Confederate Armies*, ser. 1, vol. 19, pt. 1, 25 (hereafter *OR*).
6. Monocacy National Battlefield, "Invitation to Battle."

Chapter 1

7. *OR*, ser. 1, vol. 19, pt. 1, 266–67.
8. Sypher, *History of the Pennsylvania Reserve Corps*, 57–59.
9. *Union Army*, 1:371.
10. *OR*, ser. 1, vol. 19, pt. 1, 272.
11. Ibid., 185.
12. Jamison, Military Service Records.
13. Senate of the Unite States, *Journal of the Executive Proceedings*, vol. 14, part 2, 1,063.

14. *National Republican*, Library of Congress.

15. Fold3 Database, Pension Card Index, National Archives and Records Administration.

16. Jameson Family History, Research Notes and References.

17. Todd, *American Military Equipage*, 1:38.

18. O'Brien and Diefendorf, *General Orders of the War Department*, 1:217.

19. Todd, *American Military Equipage*, 1:56.

20. U.S. War Department, *Revised United States Army Regulations of 1861*, 471–72.

21. Woodhead, *Echoes of Glory*, 189.

22. U.S. War Department, *Revised United States Army Regulations of 1861*, 481.

23. Sypher, *History of the Pennsylvania Reserve Corps*, 72–77.

24. *Union Army*, 1:370–71.

25. *OR*, ser. 1, vol. 51, pt. 1, 145–47.

26. Russell, Military Service Records.

27. *Union County Star and Lewisburg Chronicle*, Library of Congress.

28. Russell, Military Service Records.

29. Find A Grave, "John Russell."

30. Howard Lanham's "United States Army Shoulder Straps" Book Web Site, "Trousers," Revised Regulations of the Army of the United States, 1861.

31. U.S. War Department, *Revised United States Army Regulations of 1861*, 464.

32. Todd, *American Military Equipage*, 1:98.

33. U.S. War Department, *Revised United States Army Regulations of 1861*, 467.

34. Hardin, *History of the Twelfth Regiment*, 4–5.

35. *Union Army*, 1:374.

36. Hardin, *History of the Twelfth Regiment*, 110.

37. *OR*, ser. 1, vol. 51, pt. 1, 154.

38. Ibid., vol. 19, pt. 1, 186.

39. Rohm, Military Service Records.

40. Fold3 Database, Pension Card Index, National Archives and Records Administration.

41. Clark, *19th Century Card Photos Kwik Guide*, 23.

42. Hardin, *History of the Twelfth Regiment*, opposite 220.

43. O'Brien and Diefendorf, *General Orders of the War Department*, 1:217.

44. Woodhead, *Echoes of Glory*, 117, 174.

45. Sypher, *History of the Pennsylvania Reserve Corps*, 83.

46. *Union Army*, 1:370.

47. *OR*, ser. 1, vol. 51, pt. 1, 144.

48. Ibid., vol. 19, pt. 1, 273.
49. Ibid., 185.
50. Thropp, Military Service Records.
51. Fold3 Database, Pension Card Index, National Archives and Records Administration.
52. Clark, *19th Century Card Photos Kwik Guide*, 18, 21.
53. Todd, *American Military Equipage*, 1:56.
54. Bates, *History of Pennsylvania Volunteers*, 1:720–21.
55. *Union Army*, 1:371–72.
56. *OR*, ser. 1, vol. 51, pt. 1, 148.
57. Ibid., vol. 19, pt. 1, 185.
58. Snowwhite, Military Service Records.
59. DePratter, "Camp Asylum."
60. Snowwhite, Military Service Records.
61. National Archives and Records Administration, *Index to the Naturalization Records*.
62. *Harrisburg (PA) Telegraph*, "Lebanon Cadets."
63. *Lebanon (PA) Daily News*, "Bookbindery and School Books"; Ames, *Official Register of the United States*, 640.
64. Fold3 Database, Pension Card Index, National Archives and Records Administration.
65. *Hamilton (OH) Evening Journal*, "Ohio Pensions."
66. *Lebanon (PA) Daily News*, "Ernest Snowwhite"; Fold3 Database, "Graves Registration Card."
67. Clark, *19th Century Card Photos Kwik Guide*, 21.
68. U.S. War Department, *Revised United States Army Regulations of 1861*, 468–69.
69. Todd, *American Military Equipage*, 1:85; Woodhead, *Echoes of Glory*, 200.
70. U.S. War Department, *Revised United States Army Regulations of 1861*, 466.
71. Bates, *History of Pennsylvania Volunteers*, 1:756–57.
72. *Union Army*, 1:372.
73. *OR*, ser. 1, vol. 51, pt. 1, 148–49.
74. Ibid., vol. 19, pt. 1, 185.
75. Kent, Military Service Records.
76. Fold3 Database, Pension Card Index, National Archives and Records Administration.
77. *Pittsburgh (PA) Dispatch*, "A Tale of the Riots."
78. *Pittsburgh (PA) Daily Post*, "Kent"; Find A Grave, "John Milton Kent."
79. U.S. War Department, *Revised United States Army Regulations of 1861*, 465.

Chapter 2

80. *OR*, ser. 1, vol. 19, pt. 1, 221–22.

81. Nolan, *Iron Brigade*, 6–8.

82. *OR*, ser. 1, vol. 51, pt. 1, 605.

83. Herdegen, *Iron Brigade in Civil War and Memory*, 121.

84. Herdegen, *Men Stood Like Iron*, 146.

85. *Union Army*, 4: 44–45.

86. *OR*, ser. 1, vol. 19, pt. 1, 252–53.

87. Ibid., 184.

88. Fairchild, Military Service Records.

89. *Union Army*, 8:85; Herdegen, *Iron Brigade in Civil War and Memory*, 40–42.

90. City of Madison, "Forest Hill Cemetery."

91. U.S. War Department, *Revised United States Army Regulations of 1861*, 462–63.

92. Todd, *American Military Equipage*, 1:98.

93. U.S. War Department, *Revised United States Army Regulations of 1861*, 481.

94. Smith, *History of the Seventy-Sixth New York Volunteers*, 28–32.

95. *Union Army*, 2:106; Fox, *Regimental Losses in the American Civil War*, 209.

96. *OR*, ser. 1, vol. 19, pt. 1, 237–38.

97. Ibid., 184.

98. Smith, *History of the Seventy-Sixth New York Volunteers*, 348.

99. Wainwright, Military Service Records.

100. Fold3 Database, Pension Card Index, National Archives and Records Administration.

101. Hunt and Brown, *Brevet Brigadier Generals in Blue*, 641.

102. *Standard Union*, "Funeral of Col. Wainwright."

103. O'Brien and Diefendorf, *General Orders of the War Department*, 1:217.

104. U.S. War Department, *Revised United States Army Regulations of 1861*, 465.

105. Ibid., 462–63

106. Todd, *American Military Equipage*, 1:107–8

107. U.S. War Department, *Revised United States Army Regulations of 1861*, 471.

108. Todd, *American Military Equipage*, 1:78, 228–29.

109. U.S. War Department, *Revised United States Army Regulations of 1861*, 469–70; Woodhead, *Echoes of Glory*, 74–75.

110. Todd, *American Military Equipage*, 1:178–79.

111. Woodhead, *Echoes of Glory*, 180–81.

112. Phisterer, *New York in the War of the Rebellion*, 391–92.

113. *Union Army*, 2:66.

114. Raus, *Banners South*, 193–95.

115. Madill, Military Service Records.

116. American Civil War Research Database, "William A. Madill."

117. Pennsylvania Census Data—Year 1870; Pennsylvania Census Data— Year 1880.

118. *Mansfield (PA) Advertiser*, "Death of a Former Mansfield Doctor"; Tri- Counties Genealogy & History, "Wysox Cemetery."

119. Maxson, *Campfires of the Twenty-Third*, 139.

120. Todd, *American Military Equipage*, 1:71.

121. Ibid., 1:56.

122. Woodhead, *Echoes of Glory*, 174; author's collection.

123. U.S. War Department, *Revised United States Army Regulations of 1861*, 471–72.

124. Maxson, *Campfires of the Twenty-Third*, 188–89.

125. U.S. War Department, *Revised United States Army Regulations of 1861*, 469.

126. Woodhead, *Echoes of Glory*, 72–73.

127. U.S. War Department, *Revised United States Army Regulations of 1861*, 465–66; Woodhead, *Echoes of Glory*, 184–85.

128. Phisterer, *New York in the War of the Rebellion*, 440–41.

129. Jaques, *Three Years' Campaign of the Ninth*, 110.

130. *OR*, ser. 1, vol. 19, pt. 1, 261.

131. Ibid., 185.

132. Hendrickson, Military Service Records.

133. Hunt and Brown, *Brevet Brigadier Generals in Blue*, 279.

134. American Civil War Research Database, "John Hendrickson."

135. *New-York Tribune*, "General J Hendrickson Dead"; "Hendrickson"; Find A Grave, "Col John Hendrickson."

136. Adjunct General's Office, *General Orders Affecting the Volunteer Forces*, 170.

137. Woodhead, *Echoes of Glory*, 118–19.

138. Hall, *History of the Ninety-Seventh*, 284.

139. *Union Army*, 2:119.

140. Hall, *History of the Ninety-Seventh*, 87.

141. Rockwell, Military Service Records.

142. New York Division of Military and Naval Affairs, "Muster In Roll," Company E, 97th Regiment, NYSV.

143. Rockwell, Military Service Records.

144. Speer, *Portals to Hell*, 266–68.

145. American Civil War Research Database, "Soldier History: Justo O. Rockwell."

146. DePratter, "Camp Asylum."

147. Rockwell, Military Service Records.

148. Fold3 Database, Pension Card Index, National Archives and Records Administration.

149. *Seattle (WA) Post-Intelligencer*, "Notice of Nominations: Prohibition Ticket—District No. 39"; "Notice of Nominations: Prohibition Ticket—For Representative 39th District."

150. *Spokane (WA) Chronicle*, "Blushing Bride Keeps Her Name Out of Records."

151. Fold3 Database, Pension Card Index, National Archives and Records Administration.

152. *News-Herald*, "Former Resident Amid Old Scenes."

153. Clark, *19th Century Card Photos Kwik Guide*, 23.

154. Phisterer, *New York in the War of the Rebellion*, 459.

155. *Union Army*, 2:126.

156. Hartwig, *To Antietam Creek*, 392.

157. Ibid., 393.

158. *OR*, ser. 1, vol. 19, pt. 1, 185.

159. Ibid., 259.

160. Hough, *History of Duryee's Brigade*, 147–48.

161. Brandley, Military Service Records.

162. Fold3 Database, Pension Card Index, National Archives and Records Administration.

163. U.S. War Department, *Revised United States Army Regulations of 1861*, 472.

164. Todd, *American Military Equipage*, 1:228–29.

165. U.S. War Department, *Revised United States Army Regulations of 1861*, 469.

166. Howard Lanham's "United States Army Shoulder Straps" Book Web Site, "Trimmings," Revised Regulations of the Army of the United States, 1861.

Chapter 3

167. *OR*, ser. 1, vol. 19, pt. 1, 458.

168. Reid, *Ohio in the War*, 2:160–61.

169. *Union Army*, 2: 375–76.

170. *OR*, ser. 1, vol. 19, pt. 1, 461.

171. Ibid., 187.

172. Beecher, *Historical Collections of the Mahoning Valley*, 421.

173. Gillis, Military Service Records.

174. Beecher, *Historical Collections of the Mahoning Valley*, 411.

175. Ibid., 411, 421.

176. Find A Grave, "Capt Amos F Gillis."

177. Axline, Foraker and Robinson, *Official Roster of the Soldiers of the State of Ohio*, 3:80.

178. Weidman, *Artists in Ohio*, 879; Axline, Foraker and Robinson, *Official Roster of the Soldiers of the State of Ohio*, 3:80.

179. U.S. War Department, *Revised United States Army Regulations of 1861*, 462–63.

180. Ibid., 471–72.

181. Woodhead, *Echoes of Glory*, 117.

182. U.S. War Department, *Revised United States Army Regulations of 1861*, 467.

183. Reid, *Ohio in the War*, 2:202–4.

184. *Union Army*, 2:379–80.

185. *OR*, ser. 1, vol. 19, pt. 1, 461–62.

186. Ibid., 187.

187. Hamilton, Military Service Records.

188. Fold3 Database, Pension Card Index, National Archives and Records Administration.

189. *Indianapolis (IN) News*, "Minor Mentions"; *Indianapolis (IN) Journal*, "Minor Matters."

190. National Archives and Records Administration, *Application for Headstones*.

191. Axline, Foraker and Robinson, *Official Roster of the Soldiers of the State of Ohio*, 3:420.

192. Mettendorf, *Between Triumph and Disaster*, 4 and 7.

193. *Union Army*, 2:83.

194. *OR*, ser. 1, vol. 19, pt. 1, 441–42.

195. Ibid., 186.

196. National Archives and Records Administration, *Passenger Lists of Vessels Arriving*.

197. Hohle, Military Service Records.

198. American Civil War Research Database, "Soldier History: Theodore Hohle."

199. National Archives and Records Administration, *Passenger Lists of Vessels Arriving*.

200. U.S. War Department, *Revised United States Army Regulations of 1861*, 465.

201. O'Brien and Diefendorf, *General Orders of the War Department*, 1:217.

202. Todd, *American Military Equipage*, 1:56.

203. U.S. War Department, *Revised United States Army Regulations of 1861*, 462–63.

204. Woodhead, *Echoes of Glory*, 174; author's collection.

205. Todd, *American Military Equipage*, 1:98.

206. U.S. War Department, *Revised United States Army Regulations of 1861*, 472; Woodhead, *Echoes of Glory*, 175.

207. Todd, *American Military Equipage*, 1:78, 85.

208. Woodhead, *Echoes of Glory*, 74–75.

209. U.S. War Department, *Revised United States Army Regulations of 1861*, 470.

210. Ibid., 466–67.

211. Ibid., 481.

212. Bates, *History of Pennsylvania Volunteers*, 1:1,057–59.

213. *Union Army*, 1:378–79.

214. *OR*, ser. 1, vol. 19, pt. 1, 440.

215. Ibid., 186.

216. Albert, *History of the Forty-Fifth Regiment*, 224–25.

217. Scudder, Military Service Records.

218. Albert, *History of the Forty-Fifth Regiment*, 133, 239.

219. Find A Grave, "1LT George P. Scudder."

220. Clark, *19th Century Card Photos Kwik Guide*, 21.

221. U.S. War Department, *Revised United States Army Regulations of 1861*, 471–72.

222. Todd, *American Military Equipage*, 1:84.

223. U.S. War Department, *Revised United States Army Regulations of 1861*, 467; Woodhead, *Echoes of Glory*, 181.

224. Walcott, *History of the Twenty-First Regiment*, 1–2, 7–9 and 20.

225. Cole, *Massachusetts Soldiers, Sailors and Marines*, 2:594–95.

226. *OR*, ser. 1, vol. 19, pt. 1, 448.

227. Fold3 Database, "Theodore Samuel Foster."

228. Walcott, *History of the Twenty-First Regiment*, 39, 47, 49.

229. Fold3 Database, "Theodore Samuel Foster."

230. *Boston Globe*, "Dies While on Duty"; *Boston Globe*, "Funeral of Col Foster."

231. Find A Grave, "LTC Theodore Samuel Foster."

232. Turner, *Record of Service of Michigan Volunteers*, 1.

233. *Union Army*, 3:404–5.

234. *OR*, ser. 1, vol. 19, pt. 1, 427–29.

235. Ibid., 186.

236. Simpson, Military Service Records.

237. *New York Times*, "ON THE BATTLE-FIELD."

238. Simpson, Military Service Records.

239. Fold3 Database, Pension Card Index, National Archives and Records Administration.

240. *Detroit (MI) Free Press*, "Floral Hall"; "Division 1: Class 54."

241. American Civil War Research Database, "Soldier History: Hiram Simpson"; Find A Grave, "Hiram Simpson."

242. Tinder, Directory of Early Michigan Photographers, 109.

243. Lane, *Soldier's Diary*, 11.

Chapter 4

244. *OR*, ser. 1, vol. 19, pt. 1, 45.

245. Peck, Revised Roster of the Vermont Volunteers, 106.

246. *Union Army*, 1:110.

247. Benedict, *Vermont in the Civil War*, 1:175–76.

248. *OR*, ser. 1, vol. 19, pt. 1, 408.

249. Ibid., 183.

250. Aikens, Military Service Records.

251. Vermont in the Civil War, https://vermontcivilwar.org.

252. Benedict, *Vermont in the Civil War*, 1:168.

253. Todd, *American Military Equipage*, 1:70–71.

254. Woodhead, *Echoes of Glory*, 127; Howard Lanham's "United States Army Shoulder Straps" Book Web Site, "Trousers," Revised Regulations of the Army of the United States, 1861.

255. Howard Lanham's "United States Army Shoulder Straps" Book Web Site, "Uniform for Enlisted Men," Revised Regulations of the Army of the United States, 1861.

256. Woodhead, *Echoes of Glory*, 182–83.

257. U.S. War Department, *Revised United States Army Regulations of 1861*, 481.

258. Peck, Revised Roster of the Vermont Volunteers, 27–29.

259. *Union Army*, 1:108–9.

260. Benedict, *Vermont in the Civil War*, 1:122.

261. Zeller, *Second Vermont Volunteer Infantry Regiment*, 97.

262. *OR*, ser. 1, vol. 19, pt. 1, 183.

263. Edgerton, Military Service Records.

264. Vermont in the Civil War, "Francis Monroe Edgerton."

265. Wilson, *Shouts & Whispers*, 87–90.

266. *OR*, ser. 1, vol. 19, pt. 2, 382.

267. Todd, *American Military Equipage*, 1:38.

268. Woodhead, *Echoes of Glory*, 193.

269. Howard Lanham's "United States Army Shoulder Straps" Book Web Site, "Trousers," Revised Regulations of the Army of the United States, 1861.

270. O'Brien and Diefendorf, *General Orders of the War Department*, 1:217.

271. Todd, *American Military Equipage*, 1:56.

272. Howard Lanham's "United States Army Shoulder Straps" Book Web Site, "Buttons," Revised Regulations of the Army of the United States, 1861.

273. U.S. War Department, *Revised United States Army Regulations of 1861*, 471.

274. Howard Lanham's "United States Army Shoulder Straps" Book Web Site, "Trimmings," Revised Regulations of the Army of the United States, 1861.

275. *Union Army*, 3:35–36.

276. *OR*, ser. 1, vol. 19, pt. 1, 384.

277. Ibid., 183.

278. Snell, *History of Sussex and Warren Counties*, 115.

279. Wintermute, Military Service Records.

280. Wintermute, *Wintermute Family History*, 63–64.

281. Fold3 Database, Pension Card Index, National Archives and Records Administration.

282. Billings, *Hardtack and Coffee*, 204–5.

283. U.S. War Department, *Revised United States Army Regulations of 1861*, 170.

284. Woodhead, *Echoes of Glory*, 127.

285. Todd, *American Military Equipage*, 1:67.

286. U.S. War Department, *Revised United States Army Regulations of 1861*, 464.

287. Howard Lanham's "United States Army Shoulder Straps" Book Web Site, "Uniform for Enlisted Men," Revised Regulations of the Army of the United States, 1861.

288. *Union Army*, 1:431–32.

289. *OR*, ser. 1, vol. 19, pt. 1, 400–401.

290. Ibid.

291. Heitman, *Historical Register and Dictionary*, 279.

292. Campbell, Military Service Records.

293. Clark, *19ᵗʰ Century Card Photos Kwik Guide*, 23.

294. Woodhead, *Echoes of Glory*, 111.

295. O'Brien and Diefendorf, *General Orders of the War Department*, 1:177.

296. Howard Lanham's "United States Army Shoulder Straps" Book Web Site, "Various Components: Cravat or Stock," Revised Regulations of the Army of the United States, 1861.

297. Woodhead, *Echoes of Glory*, 185–87.

298. U.S. War Department, *Revised United States Army Regulations of 1861*, 466.

299. *Union Army*, 2:71.

300. *OR*, ser. 1, vol. 19, pt. 1, 399.

301. Ibid., 183.

302. Erskine Rich, Military Service Records, Company H, 84th New York Volunteer Infantry, National Archives.

303. Erskine Rich, Military Service Records, Company I, 31st New York Volunteer Infantry, National Archives.

304. New York State Military Museum and Veterans Research Center, "Annual Report of the Adjutant-General."

305. GW Green Wood Cemetery, "Civil War Biographies: Rice-Ryker."

306. Ridgeway Civil War Research Center, "Civil War Buttons: New York State Button"; author's collection.

307. U.S. War Department, *Revised United States Army Regulations of 1861*, 468.

308. Todd, *American Military Equipage*, 1:228.

309. Howard Lanham's "United States Army Shoulder Straps" Book Web Site, "Sword Components: Sword-Belt Plate," Revised Regulations of the Army of the United States, 1861.

310. U.S. War Department, *Revised United States Army Regulations of 1861*, 469.

311. Todd, *American Military Equipage*, 1:180; Woodhead, *Echoes of Glory*, 74–75.

312. Howard Lanham's "United States Army Shoulder Straps" Book Web Site, "Sword Components: Sword-Belt Plate," Revised Regulations of the Army of the United States, 1861.

313. *Union Army*, 2:71.

314. *OR*, ser. 1, vol. 19, pt. 1, 396–97.

315. Ibid., 183.

316. Lemon, Military Service Records.

317. Barnes and U.S. Army, Office of the Surgeon General, *Medical and Surgical History of the War*, 2:313.

318. U.S. War Department, *Revised United States Army Regulations of 1861*, 462–63.

319. Howard Lanham's "United States Army Shoulder Straps" Book Web Site, "Badges to Distinguish Rank: Shoulder Straps," Revised Regulations of the Army of the United States, 1861.

320. *OR*, series 1, vol. 51, part 1, 839–40.

Chapter 5

321. *Union Army*, 2:410; Ohio Civil War Central, "87th Regiment Ohio Volunteer Infantry."

322. Carman, *Maryland Campaign of September 1862*, 1:250.

323. *OR*, ser. 1, vol. 19, pt. 1, 549.

324. Hunt and Brown, *Brevet Brigadier Generals in Blue*, 30.

325. U.S. War Department, *Revised United States Army Regulations of 1861*, 480.

326. Reid, *Ohio in the War*, 1:830.

327. Clark, *19th Century Card Photos Kwik Guide*, 23.

328. Reid, *Ohio in the War*, 1:830.

329. U.S. War Department, *Revised United States Army Regulations of 1861*, 465.

330. Howard Lanham's "United States Army Shoulder Straps" Book Web Site, "Uniform for Commissioned Officers" Revised Regulations of the Army of the United States, 1861; "Badges to Distinguish Rank: Shoulder Straps," Revised Regulations of the Army of the United States, 1861.

331. Todd, *American Military Equipage*, 1:56.

332. *Union Army*, 2:141.

333. *OR*, ser. 1, vol. 19, pt. 1, 532–40.

334. Ibid., 549.

335. Frye, *History and Tour Guide*, 38.

336. Armstrong, Military Service Records.

337. Eisenschiml, *Vermont General*, 30–31; Hampton University, "Samuel Chapman Armstrong."

338. U.S. War Department, *Revised United States Army Regulations of 1861*, 462–63.

339. Howard Lanham's "United States Army Shoulder Straps" Book Web Site, "Buttons," Revised Regulations of the Army of the United States, 1861.

340. Peck, *Revised Roster of the Vermont Volunteers*, 338.

341. Benedict, *Vermont in the Civil War*, 2:186–90.

342. Ibid., 2:194–95.

343. *OR*, ser. 1, vol. 19, pt. 1, 549.

344. Peck, *Revised Roster of the Vermont Volunteers*, 339–42.

345. Vermont in the Civil War "Jarvis, Charles."

346. Fold3 Database, Charles Jarvis, Military Service Records, Company D, 9th Vermont Volunteer Infantry.

347. Howard Lanham's "United States Army Shoulder Straps" Book Web Site, "Badges to Distinguish Rank: Shoulder Straps," Revised Regulations of the Army of the United States, 1861.

348. Willson, *Disaster, Struggle; Triumph*, 19–21.
349. *Union Army*, 2:142.
350. Murray, *Redemption of the "Harpers Ferry Cowards,"* 26–27.
351. *OR*, ser. 1, vol. 19, pt. 1, 549.
352. Green, Military Service Records.
353. Fold3 Database, Pension Card Index, National Archives and Records Administration.
354. Find A Grave, "Sgt Fayette Green."
355. Woodhead, *Echoes of Glory*, 191.
356. U.S. War Department, *Revised United States Army Regulations of 1861*, 463.
357. Todd, *American Military Equipage*, 1:65.
358. *Union Army*, 2:130.
359. *OR*, ser. 1, vol. 19, pt. 1, 527.
360. Ibid., 549.
361. New York State Military Museum and Veterans Research Center, "Roster of the One Hundred and Eleventh Infantry."
362. Servis, Military Service Records.
363. Fold3 Database, Pension Card Index, National Archives and Records Administration.
364. Find A Grave, "Howard Servis."
365. Howard Lanham's "United States Army Shoulder Straps" Book Web Site, "Trousers," Revised Regulations of the Army of the United States, 1861; O'Brien and Diefendorf, *General Orders of the War Department*, 1:217.
366. U.S. War Department, *Revised United States Army Regulations of 1861*, 467.
367. Todd, *American Military Equipage*, 1:88–89.
368. Silo, *115ᵗʰ New York in the Civil War*, 8.
369. *Union Army*, 2:132.
370. Clark, *Iron Hearted Regiment*, 15–16.
371. *OR*, ser. 1, vol. 19, pt. 1, 549.
372. Drake, Military Service Records.
373. Fold3 Database, Pension Card Index, National Archives and Records Administration.
374. Clark, *19ᵗʰ Century Card Photos Kwik Guide*, 23.
375. Woodhead, *Echoes of Glory*, 174.
376. U.S. War Department, *Revised United States Army Regulations of 1861*, 464; Woodhead, *Echoes of Glory*, 236.
377. Todd, *American Military Equipage*, 1:65; Woodhead, *Echoes of Glory*, 180–81.

Epilogue

378. *OR*, ser. 1, vol. 19, pt. 1, 183–87.
379. Ibid., 549.
380. Frye, *History and Tour Guide*, 65.

Bibliography

Primary Sources

Adjunct General's Office. *General Orders Affecting the Volunteer Forces: 1864*. Washington, D.C.: Government Printing Office, 1865.

Albert, Allen D., ed. *History of the Forty-Fifth Regiment Pennsylvania Veteran Volunteer Infantry, 1861–1865*. Williamsport, PA: Grit Publishing Company, 1912.

Ames, J.G. *Official Register of the United States, Containing a List of Officers and Employees in the Civil, Military and Naval Service*, Vol. 1. Washington, D.C.: Government Printing Office, 1887.

Aubin, J. Harris. *Register of the Military Order of the Loyal Legion of the United States*. Boston, MA: Commandery of the State of Massachusetts, 1906.

Axline, H.A., Joseph B. Foraker and James S. Robinson. *Official Roster of the Soldiers of the State of Ohio in the War of the Rebellion*. Vol. 3, *21ˢᵗ–36ᵗʰ Regiments Infantry*. Cincinnati: Ohio Valley Publishing and Manufacturing Company, 1886.

Barnes, Joseph K., and U.S. Army, Office of the Surgeon General. *The Medical and Surgical History of the War of the Rebellion*. Vol. 2, Part 3. Washington, D.C.: US Government Printing Office, 1870.

Billings, John D. *Hard Tack and Coffee*. Boston, MA: George M. Smith & Company, 1888.

Carman, Ezra A. *The Maryland Campaign of September 1862*. Vol. 1, *South Mountain*. Edited by Dr. Thomas G. Clemens. New York: Savas Beatie LLC, 2010.

Clark, James H. *The Iron Hearted Regiment Being an Account of the Battles, Marches and Gallant Deeds Performed by the 115th Regiment N.Y. Vols*. Albany, NY: J. Munsell, 1865.

Eisenschiml, Otto, ed. *Vermont General: The Unusual War Experiences of Edward Hastings Ripley, 1862–1865*. New York: Devin-Adair Company, 1960.

Hall, Isaac. *History of the Ninety-Seventh New York Volunteers, (Conkling Rifles), in the War for the Union*. Utica, NY: L.C. Childs & Son, 1896.

Hardin, Martin Davis. *History of the Twelfth Regiment Pennsylvania Volunteer Corps*. New York: published by the author, 1890.

Hough, Franklin B. *History of Duryee's Brigade, During the Campaign in Virginia under Gen. Pope, and in Maryland under Gen. McClellan, in the Summer and Autumn of 1862*. Albany, NY: J. Munsell, 78th Street, 1864.

Jaques, John W. *Three Years' Campaign of the Ninth, N.Y.S.M., During the Southern Rebellion*. New York: Hilton & Company Publishers, 1865.

Lane, David. *A Soldier's Diary: The Story of a Volunteer, 1862–1865*. Jackson, MI: published by author, 1905.

Maxson, William P. *Campfires of the Twenty-Third: Sketches of the Camplife, Marches and Battles of the Twenty-Third Regiment, N.Y.V.* New York: Davies & Kent Printers, 1863.

Military Order of the Loyal Legion. *Journal of the Proceedings of the Forty-first Annual Meeting of the Commandery-in-Chief*. Philadelphia, PA: Military Order of the Loyal Legion of the United States, 1926.

National Archives and Records Administration. *Application for Headstones for U.S. Military Veterans, 1925–1941*. Microfilm Publication M1916, 134 rolls. ARC ID: 596118. Records of the Office of the Quartermaster General, Record Ground 92. Washington, D.C.

————. *Index to the Naturalization Records of the U.S. Supreme Court of the District of Columbia, 1802–1909*. Microfilm Serial: M1827, Microfilm Roll 1. Washington, D.C.

————. *Passenger Lists of Vessels Arriving at New York, New York, 1820–1897*. Microfilm Publication M237, 675 rolls. NAI: 6256867. Records of the U.S. Customs Service, Record Group 36. Washington, D.C.

O'Brien, Thomas M., and Oliver Diefendorf. *General Orders of the War Department, Embracing the Years 1861, 1862 & 1863. Adapted Specifically for the Use of the Army and Navy of the United States*. Vols. 1–2. New York: Derby & Miller, No. 5 Spruce Street, 1864.

Peck, Theodore S., Adjutant General. *Revised Roster of the Vermont Volunteers and Lists of Vermonters Who Served in the Army and Navy of the United States during the War of the Rebellion, 1861–66*. Montpelier, VT: Press of the Watchman Publishing Company, Publishers and Printers, 1892.

Pennsylvania Census Data—Year 1880. Census Place: Archbald, Lackawanna, Pennsylvania, Roll: 1137, page 188B. Enumeration District 033.

Pennsylvania Census Data—Year 1870. Census Place: Dushore, Sullivan, Pennsylvania, Roll: M593_1453, page 26B. Family History Library Film, 552952.

Senate of the United States. *Journal of the Executive Proceedings of the Senate of the United States*. Vol. 14, Part 2. Washington, D.C.: Government Printing Office, 1866.

Smith, A.P. *History of the Seventy-Sixth New York Volunteers; What It Endured and Accomplished*. Cortland, NY: Truair, Smith & Miles, Printer, 1867.

Sypher, J.R. *History of the Pennsylvania Reserve Corps: A Complete Record of the Organization*. Lancaster, PA: Elias Barr & Company, 1865.

The Union Army. Vols I–X. Wilmington, NC: Broadfoot, 1997. First published in 1908 by Federal Publishing Company.

U.S. War Department. *Revised United States Army Regulations of 1861, with an Appendix Containing the Changed and Laws Affecting Army Regulations and Articles of War to June 25, 1863*. Washington, D.C.: Government Printing Office, 1863.

U.S. War Department, John Sheldon Moody, Calvin Duvall Cowles, Frederick Caryton Ainsworth et al. *The War of the Rebellion: A Compilation of the Official Records of the Union and Confederate Armies*. Series 1, vol. 51. Washington, D.C.: Government Printing Office, 1897.

———. *The War of the Rebellion: A Compilation of the Official Records of the Union and Confederate Armies*. Series 1, vol. 19. Washington, D.C.: Government Printing Office, 1889.

Walcott, Charles F. *History of the Twenty-First Regiment Massachusetts Volunteers in the War for the Preservation of the Union, 1861–1865*. Boston, MA: Houghton Mifflin and Company, 1882.

Willson, Arabella M. *Disaster, Struggle; Triumph: The Adventures of 1000 "Boys in Blue," from August 1862, to June 1865*. Albany, NY: Argus Company, Printers, 1870.

Wilson, Nancy D. *Shouts & Whispers: The Civil War Correspondence of D.D. Priest of Mount Holly, Vermont*. Manchester Center, VT: Shire Press, 2011.

Newspapers

Boston Globe. "Dies While on Duty." February 7, 1910, page 13.

———. "Funeral of Col Foster." February 9, 1910, page 7.

Detroit (MI) Free Press. "Division 1: Class 54." September 23, 1868, page 1.

———. "Floral Hall." September 18, 1868, page 1.

Hamilton (OH) Evening Journal. "Ohio Pensions." March 29, 1892, page 1.

Harrisburg (PA) Telegraph. "Lebanon Cadets." September 22, 1869, page 3.

Indianapolis (IN) Journal. "Minor Matters." August 5, 1887, page 2.

Indianapolis (IN) News. "Minor Mentions." August 4, 1887, page 1.

Lebanon (PA) Daily News. "Bookbindery and School Books." January 16, 1873, page 2.

———. "Ernest Snowwhite." December 23, 1902, page 4.

Mansfield (PA) Advertiser. "Death of a Former Mansfield Doctor." September 25, 1889, page 3.

National Republican (Washington, D.C.). March 6, 1867. Library of Congress, Chronicling America: Historic American Newspapers. https://chroniclingamerica.loc.gov/lccn/sn86053571/1867-03-06/ed-1/seq-3.

News-Herald (Franklin, Pennsylvania). "Former Resident Amid Old Scenes." July 14, 1913, page 2.

New York Times. "ON THE BATTLE-FIELD, Sunday Night, Sept. 14, 1862." September 17, 1862, page 1.

New-York Tribune. "General J Hendrickson Dead." June 30, 1902, page 7.

———. "Hendrickson." July 2, 1902, page 9.

Pittsburgh (PA) Daily Post. "Kent." July 4, 1891, page 5.

Pittsburgh (PA) Dispatch. "A Tale of the Riots." September 6, 1891, page 18.

Seattle (WA) Post-Intelligencer. "Notice of Nominations: Prohibition Ticket—District No. 39." October 27, 1894, page 6.

———. "Notice of Nominations: Prohibition Ticket—For Representative 39th District." October 25, 1896, page 19.

Spokane (WA) Chronicle. "Blushing Bride Keeps Her Name Out of Records." August 21, 1930, page 17.

Standard Union (Brooklyn, New York). "Funeral of Col. Wainwright." October 19, 1895, page 2.

Union County Star and Lewisburg Chronicle. May 31, 1864, page 1. Library of Congress, Chronicling America: Historic American Newspapers. https://chroniclingamerica.loc.gov/lccn/sn85038443/1864-05-31/ed-1/seq-1.

Military Service Records

Aikens, Joseph. Military Service Records, Company D, 4th Vermont Volunteer Infantry, National Archives.

Armstrong, Samuel. Military Service Records, Company D, 125th New York State Volunteer Infantry, National Archives.

Banning, Henry B. Military Service Records, Field and Staff, 87th Ohio Volunteer Infantry, National Archives.

Brandley, Patrick W. Military Service Records, Company H, 105th New York Volunteer Infantry, National Archives.

Campbell, William J. Military Service Records, Company A, 95th Pennsylvania Volunteer Infantry, National Archives.

Drake, Ezra. Military Service Records, Company F, 115th New York State Volunteer Infantry, National Archives.

Edgerton, Francis. Military Service Records, Company B, 2nd Vermont Volunteer Infantry, National Archives.

Fairchild, Lucius. Military Service Records, Field and Staff, 2nd Wisconsin Volunteer Infantry, National Archives.

Foster, Theodore Samuel. Military Service Records, Company F, 21st Massachusetts Volunteer Infantry, accessed December 21, 2019. https://www.fold3.com/image/272/525511168.

Gillis, Amos F. Military Service Records, Company B, 23rd Ohio Volunteer Infantry, National Archives.

Green, Fayette. Military Service Records, Company E, 126th New York State Volunteer Infantry, National Archives.

Hamilton, Mathias. Military Service Records, Company I, 30th Ohio Volunteer Infantry, National Archives.

Hendrickson, John. Military Service Records, Field and Staff, 83rd New York Volunteer Infantry, National Archives.

Hohle, Theodore. Military Service Records, Company H, 46th New York Volunteer Infantry, National Archives.

Jamison, Albion B. Military Service Records, Company A, 6th Pennsylvania Reserve Infantry (35th Infantry) Volunteer Infantry, National Archives.

Jarvis, Charles. Military Service Records, Company D, 9th Vermont Volunteer Infantry, accessed December 24, 2019. https://www.fold3.com/image/272/311504123.

Kent, John M. Military Service Records, Company I, 8th Pennsylvania Reserve Infantry (37th Infantry) Volunteer Infantry, National Archives.

Lemon, George F. Military Service Records, Field and Staff, 32nd New York Volunteer Infantry, National Archives.

Madill, William A. Military Service Records, Field and Staff, 23rd New York Volunteer Infantry, National Archives.

Rich, Erskine. Military Service Records, Company I, 31st New York Volunteer Infantry, National Archives.

Rich, Erskine. Military Service Records, Company H, 84th New York Volunteer Infantry, National Archives.

Rockwell, Justus O. Military Service Records, Company E, 97th New York Volunteer Infantry, National Archives.

Rohm, John G. Military Service Records, Company K, 12th Pennsylvania Reserve Infantry (41st Infantry) Volunteer Infantry, National Archives.

Russell, J. Woods. Military Service Records, Company A, 5th Pennsylvania Reserve Infantry (34th Infantry) Volunteer Infantry, National Archives.

Scudder, George P. Military Service Records, Company F, 45th Pennsylvania Volunteer Infantry, National Archives.

Servis, Howard. Military Service Records, Company B, 111th New York State Volunteer Infantry, National Archives.

Simpson, Hiram. Military Service Records, Company K, 17th Michigan Volunteer Infantry, National Archives.

Snowwhite, Ernest. Military Service Records, Company C, 7th Pennsylvania Reserve Infantry (33rd Infantry) Volunteer Infantry, National Archives.

Thropp, Isaiah, Jr. Military Service Records, Company K, 4th Pennsylvania Reserve Infantry (33rd Infantry) Volunteer Infantry, National Archives.

Wainwright, William P. Military Service Records, Field and Staff, 76th New York Volunteer Infantry, National Archives.

Wintermute, Andrew. Military Service Records, Company B, 2nd New Jersey Volunteer Infantry, National Archives.

Secondary Sources

Bates, Samuel P. *History of Pennsylvania Volunteers, 1861–1865.* Vol. 1. Harrisburg, PA: B. Singerly, State Printer, 1869.

Beecher, W.A. *Historical Collections of the Mahoning Valley.* Youngstown, OH: Mahoning Valley Historical Society, 1876.

Benedict, George G. *Vermont in the Civil War. A History of the Part Taken by the Vermont Soldiers and Sailors in the War for the Union, 1861–5.* Vols. 1–2. Burlington, VT: Free Press Association, 1886–88.

Clark, Gary W. *19th Century Card Photos Kwik Guide: A Step-by-Step Guide to Identifying and Dating: Cartes de Vistite and Cabinet Cards*. Wichita, KS: PhotoTree.com, 2013.

Cole, Charles H. *Massachusetts Soldiers, Sailors and Marines in the Civil War*. Vol. 2. Norwood, MA: Norwood Press, 1931.

Darrah, William C. *Cartes de Visite: In Nineteenth Century Photography*. Gettysburg, PA: W.C. Darrah Publisher, 1981.

Dyer, Frederick H. *Compendium of the War of the Rebellion*. Vol. 2. Dayton, OH: Morningside Bookshop, 1978.

Foreman, Amanda. *A World on Fire: Britain's Crucial Role in the American Civil War*. New York: Random House Publishing, 2010.

Fox, William F. *Regimental Losses in the American Civil War, 1861–1865*. Albany, NY: Albany Publishing Company, 1889.

Frye, Dennis E. *History and Tour Guide of Stonewall Jackson's Battle of Harpers Ferry, September 12–15, 1862*. N.p.: Blue and Gray Publications, 2012.

Hartwig, D. Scott. *To Antietam Creek: The Maryland Campaign of September 1862*. Baltimore, MD: Johns Hopkins University Press, 2012.

Heitman, Francis B. *Historical Register and Dictionary of the United States Army from Its Organization September 29, 1789 to March 2, 1903*. Washington, D.C.: Government Printing Office, 1903.

Herdegen, Lance J. *The Iron Brigade in Civil War and Memory*. El Dorado Hills, CA: Savas Beatie, 2012.

———. *The Men Stood Like Iron: How the Iron Brigade Won Its Name*. Bloomington: Indiana University Press, 2005.

Hunt, Roger D., and Jack R. Brown. *Brevet Brigadier Generals in Blue*. Gaithersburg, MD: Olde Soldier Books, 1990.

Mettendorf, Ernest. *Between Triumph and Disaster: The History of the 46th New York Infantry 1861 to 1865*. Eden, NY: self-published, 2012.

Murray, R.L. *The Redemption of the "Harpers Ferry Cowards": The Story of the 111th and 126th New York State Volunteer Regiments at Gettysburg*. Wolcott, NY: R.L. Murray Publisher, 1994.

Nolan, Alan T. *The Iron Brigade: A Military History*. Bloomington: Indiana University Press, 1994.

Phisterer, Frederick. *New York in the War of the Rebellion, 1861 to 1865*. Albany, NY: Weed, Parsons & Company, 1890.

Radcliffe, George E. *Governor Thomas H. Hicks of Maryland and the Civil War*. Baltimore, MD: Johns Hopkins Press, 1901.

Raus, Edmund J., Jr. *Banners South: A Northern Community at War*. Kent, OH: Kent State University Press, 2005.

Reid, Whitelaw. *Ohio in the War: Her Statesmen, Her Generals, and Soldiers*. Vol 1, *The History of Ohio during the War and the Lives of Her Generals*. Cincinnati, OH: Robert Clarke Company, 1895.

————. *Ohio in the War: Her Statesmen, Her Generals, and Soldiers*. Vol. 2, *The History of Her Regiments and Other Military Organizations*. Cincinnati, OH: Moore, Wilstach & Baldwin, 1898.

Silo, Mark. *The 115th New York in the Civil War: A Regimental History*. Jefferson, NC: McFarland & Company, 2007.

Snell, James P. *History of Sussex and Warren Counties, New Jersey*. Philadelphia, PA: Everts & Peck, 1881.

Speer, Lonnie R. *Portals to Hell: Military Prisons in the Civil War*. Mechanicsburg, PA: Stackpole Books, 1997.

Todd, Frederick P. *American Military Equipage, 1851–1872*. Vol. 1. Providence, RI: Company of Military Historians, 1974.

Turner, George H. *Record of Service of Michigan Volunteers in the Civil War, 1861–1865: Seventeenth Michigan Infantry*. Kalamazoo, MI: Ihling Bros. & Everard, Stationers, Printers and Publishers, 1905.

Weidman, Jeffrey. *Artists in Ohio, 1787–1900: A Biographical Dictionary*. Kent, OH: Kent State University Press, 2000.

Wintermute, J.P. *The Wintermute Family History*. Delaware, OH: Champlin Press, 1900.

Woodhead, Henry, ed. *Echoes of Glory: Arms and Equipment of the Union*. Alexandria, VA: Time-Life Books, 1991.

Zeller, Paul. *The Second Vermont Volunteer Infantry Regiment, 1861–1865*. Jefferson, NC: McFarland & Company, 2002.

Primary Source Websites

American Civil War Research Database. "Personnel Directory." Consulted regularly throughout writing. http://www.civilwardata.com.

Antietam on the Web. Consulted regularly throughout writing. http://antietam.aotw.org.

Fold3 Database. "Graves Registration Card." https://www.fold3.com.

Howard Lanham's "United States Army Shoulder Straps" Book Web Site. Revised Regulations for the Army of the United States, 1861. Consulted regularly throughout writing. http://howardlanham.tripod.com.

National Archives and Records Administration. Pension Card Index. www.fold3.com.

New York Division of Military and Naval Affairs. "Muster In Roll," Company E, 97th Regiment, NYSV. https://dmna.ny.gov/historic/reghist/civil/MusterRolls/Infantry/97thInf_NYSV_MusterRoll.pdf.

New York State Military Museum and Veterans Research Center. "Annual Report of the Adjutant-General of the State of New York. For the Year of 1900." http://dmna.ny.gov/historic/reghist/civil/rosters/Infantry/39th_Infantry_CW_Roster.pdf.

———. "Roster of the One Hundred and Eleventh Infantry." https://dmna.ny.gov/historic/reghist/civil/rosters/Infantry/111th_Infantry_CW_Roster.pdf.

Secondary Source Websites

City of Madison. "Forest Hill Cemetery." https://crystal.cityofmadison.com.

DePratter, Chester, PhD. "Camp Asylum." South Carolina Institute of Archaeology and Anthropology, University of South Carolina–Columbia. www.columbiasc.net/depts/city-council/docs/old_downloads/08_06_2013_Agenda_Items/Camp_Asylum_for_Council.pdf.

Find A Grave. Consulted regularly throughout writing. https://www.findagrave.com.

GW Green Wood Cemetery. "Civil War Biographies: Rice-Ryker." https://www.green-wood.com.

Hampton University. "Samuel Chapman Armstrong." http://www.hamptonu.edu.

The Jameson Family History, Research Notes and References—Jameson-Church-Duke-Bower Families. http://www.jamesonfamily.org.

Monocacy National Battlefield. "An Invitation to Battle." https://www.nps.gov.

Ohio Civil War Central. "87th Regiment Ohio Volunteer Infantry (Three Months Service)." http://www.www.ohiocivilwarcentral.com.

Ridgeway Civil War Research Center. "Civil War Buttons." http://www.relicman.com.

Tinder, David V. Directory of Early Michigan Photographers. William L. Clements Library, University of Michigan. https://clements.umich.edu/files/tinder_directory.pdf.

Tri-Counties Genealogy & History. "Wysox Cemetery." https://www.joycetice.com.

Vermont in the Civil War. Consulted regularly throughout writing. https://vermontcivilwar.org.

Index

G

H

R

ABOUT THE AUTHORS

A longtime student of American history and the Civil War, MATTHEW BORDERS holds a BA in U.S. history and an MS in historic preservation. He has worked as a National Park Service ranger at Antietam National Battlefield, as well as a historian and battlefield surveyor for the National Park Service's American Battlefield Protection Program. He is also a Certified Battlefield Guide at Antietam and Harpers Ferry. Currently, Matthew is a park ranger at Monocacy National Battlefield in Frederick, Maryland, and president of the Frederick County Civil War Round Table. He, with fellow Antietam guide Joe Stahl, published *Faces of Union Soldiers at Antietam*, the first book in the *Faces of Union Soldiers* series in 2019. That same year, Matthew was honored to be the recipient of the Save Historic Antietam Foundation's Dr Joseph Harsh Award for his research topic: The Loudoun Valley Campaign of 1862: McClellan's Final Advance.

JOSEPH W. STAHL retired from the Institute for Defense Analyses, where he authored or coauthored more than fifty reports on defense issues. Since his retirement, he has become a volunteer and NPS Licensed Battlefield Guide at Antietam and Harpers Ferry. He grew up in St. Louis. He received BS and MS degrees from Missouri University of Science and Technology and an MBA from Washington University in St. Louis. He is a member of the Company of Military Historians, Save Historic Antietam Foundation (SHAF) and Hagerstown Civil War Round Table. He has spoken to various Civil War groups, including the Northern Virginia Relic Hunters; South

Mountain Coin and Relic Club; the Rappahannock, York, Chambersburg and Hagerstown Round Tables; Chambersburg Civil War Tours; SHAF; and the NPS Antietam. In addition, Joe has authored more than two dozen articles about items in his collections for *Gettysburg Magazine*, the *Washington Times*'s Civil War Page, *Manuscripts*, *America's Civil War*, *Military Collector & Historian*, the *Journal of the Company of Military Historians*, the *Civil War Historian* and the *Skirmish Line* of the North-South Skirmish Association. Displays of items from of his collection have won awards at several Civil War shows. He has been a member of the North-South Skirmish Association for more than twenty-five years and has shot Civil War–type muskets, carbines and revolvers in both individual and team competitions.